Wisdom

Making Good Choices with Imperfect Knowledge

BRENT MUIRHEAD, Ph.D.

No portion of this book may be copied, photocopied, transmitted or stored electronically or otherwise without the express permission of the publisher and authors, except for small references for the purpose of reviewing the book online or in print. To obtain permission, please contact:

DID Media
952 Wayside St.
Cornelia, GA 30531

To contact the author:

Brent Muirhead, Ph.D.
11190 Indian Village Drive
Alpharetta, GA 30022

Published August 2011

1 2 3 4 5 6 7 8 9 0

ISBN # 978-0-9846533-0-0
Printed and distributed in the US by Lightning Source, Inc.
Cover design by Digital Impact Design, Inc., Cornelia, Georgia 30531

US $24.95

DOM

Making

Good

Choices

with

Imperfect

Knowledge

Table of Contents

Part One: Wisdom xii

Chapter One: What is wisdom?. 1

Part Two: Creating 8

Chapter Two: Encouraging Creativity. 9

Chapter Three: Creativity Challenges In Education 15

Chapter Four: Improving Creativity 21

Chapter Five: Becoming Indispensable. 26

Chapter Six: Talent Alone Is Never Enough 30

Chapter Seven: Resiliency 32

Chapter Eight: Helping Others 34

Part Three: Reaching 38

Chapter Nine: Setting Goals 39

Chapter Ten: Encouraging People's Dreams. 43

Chapter Eleven: Why is it difficult to learn from mistakes? 45

Chapter Twelve: The Value of Pessimism 49

Chapter Thirteen: Dealing With Uncertainty 52

Part Four: Learning. 54

Chapter Fourteen: Boring Education 55

Chapter Fifteen: Meaningful Learning 59

Chapter Sixteen: Teachers 61

Chapter Seventeen: Educational Goals. 63

Chapter Eighteen: Higher Education 66

Chapter Nineteen: Online University Dialogs 69

Chapter Twenty: Doctoral Studies. 72

Chapter Twenty-One: Writing Skills 74

Chapter Twenty-Two: Creative Writing 78

Part Five: Seeing 82

Chapter Twenty-Three: Science Fiction Insights 83

Chapter Twenty-Four: Blogs 87

Chapter Twenty-Five: Blog Popularity 89

Chapter Twenty-Six: Children's Television Shows. 92

Chapter Twenty-Seven: Media Stars 94

Part Six: Being 96

Chapter Twenty-Eight: Social Conformity 97

Chapter Twenty-Nine: Positive Psychology 100

Chapter Thirty: The Rise of the Mega Church 103

Chapter Thirty-One: Where Are Today's Leaders. 107

Chapter Thirty-Two: Conclusion 110

Notes 115

Bibliography 122

"One of the hallmarks of wisdom, what distinguishes it so sharply from 'mere' intelligence, is the ability to exercise good judgment in the face of imperfect knowledge."

STEPHEN S. HALL

Wisdom

1 What is Wisdom?

isdom is a word that seems a bit old-fashioned today; why is that? After all, wisdom involves knowledge, insight, and judgment. One who is wise is considered to have discernment for what is true, right, or lasting and to exercise common sense and good judgment. However, descriptions of outstanding people these days are more apt to include words like *quick*, or *sharp*, or *flexible*. Certainly, a wise person can be quick, sharp, and flexible, but it seems we tend to shy away from *wise* or *wisdom*, perhaps because those terms do not sound as youthful as the others. Well, it is, perhaps, time for us to begin to bring the words *wise* and *wisdom* back into favor.

A good place to start examining the nature and necessity of wisdom is in the all-important area of decision-making. In many ways, decision-making—because in matters both large and small, it is of universal and daily concern—is big business. Self-help books and television-and-radio talk shows spend a lot of time focusing on the topic as they deliver information regarding, basically, how to make decisions on a wide range of subjects, from financial investing to how to deal with marital problems to how to save the world's economies.

Daily, our choices impact our lives. Decisions made too quickly can cause problems and have far-reaching negative consequences. Of course, some decisions can be made quickly without causing difficulties, and a major factor in good decision-making is knowing how to set priorities, how to separate that which is truly urgent from that which is not. The tendency to devote constant attention to pressing daily matters can direct time and energy away from tasks that support and affirm the pursuit of important major goals. For instance, people who do not find the time to reflect upon and then decide on how best to spend their income and make a plan to, say, save money each month for a down payment on a home, may not ever be able to make their dream of a new home come true.

Of course, the reason we may delay making the decision to save money and then implement our plan it is that on some level we realize how much more complicated the situation is than just planning and doing. Perhaps other financial obligations are a drain. Maybe we have doubts regarding the stability of the relationship that has made us want to have a home in the first place. Putting ourselves in wisdom mode, so to speak, in order to deal with this situation would begin as we decide that we need to give all the factors that enter into the plan further consideration and then, if we decide we do want to pursue the goal of buying a home, we will need to develop detailed financial plans to save the money we will need.

Being open to new perspectives and being able to consider intelligently whether and when to make an immediate decision versus gathering more information are important features of wisdom. Making hasty decisions or assumptions can be financially costly and create conflicts in relationships. Such assumptions can be embarrassing in social situations, too. At a graduation ceremony years ago, I told a newly married colleague of mine that I was glad to see his mother there, referring to the woman that, as it turned out, was not his mother at all, but his bride. I learned a valuable lesson that day regarding making assumptions about couples.

So, experience may aid in gathering wisdom, and perhaps that is one reason the words *wisdom* and *wise* may carry a sense that they are not ordinarily attributes of the very young.

Let's consider what some other characteristics of those who are wise might be, in the interest of considering which of those traits we may want to emulate or gain for ourselves.

In Stephen Hall's *Wisdom: From Philosophy to Neuroscience*, he discusses investigations into the characteristics of those considered wise. Hall identifies eight pillars of wisdom:

Eight Pillars of Wisdom from *Wisdom: Fro*

❶ Emotion Regulation - researchers have found that older individuals will focus less on negative thoughts, place a greater value on relationships and demonstrate resilience to quickly bounce back from disappoints and adversity.

❷ Knowing What is Important - those who understand what is valuable to them and have learned to make consistently make decisions to affirm their values and beliefs. Individuals who are capable of filtering information and having the emotional calm and patience to make the best choices. The choices transcend immediate gratification or economic goals and often center on achieving relational objectives.

❸ Moral Judgment - older people understand how life is fragile, acquired emotional resilience and learn to savor each day and enables the individual to have a clear perspective on what is important in their life.

❹ Compassion - the ability to be empathic and share to a degree in their suffering and demonstrate a deep concern for them. The concept requires the ability to step outside one's own self-oriented life and seek to understand another's perspective.

❺ Humility - CEOs who have narcissistic traits will be poor leaders who will make poor decisions and place their fame and fortune before the good of their companies. In contrast, leaders who are professionally driven and possess genuine humility can create great companies. Hall observes that these wise leaders "...acknowledge limitations and mistakes, an openness

So, those who are considered wise may regulate their emotions, know what is important, exercise moral judgment, be compassionate, possess humility, be altruistic and patient, and have the ability to deal with uncertainty. How often have you worked with individuals who displayed the majority of these wisdom characteristics? Which ones can you claim as realities or possibilities for your own life?

WISDOM: *Making Good Choices with Imperfect Knowledge*

Philosophy to Neuroscience by Stephen Hall

to new ideas and new contradictory knowledge, a knack for avoiding self-aggrandizement, an ability to keep one's achievements in perspective, and the kind of self-aware self-perception that perceives both strengths and weaknesses."

6 Altruism - researchers have found in experiments that social interaction can be influenced by altruistic individuals who punish those who fail to make contributions to group projects. They strive for cooperation but are willing to make sacrifices and punish the loafers or cheaters in the group. The action represents the potential for social justice in altruism by resisting those are greedy and have an entitlement attitude.

7 Patience - the ability to have a creative and positive vision of the future enables people to have self-control. An optimistic view of the future encourages people to have the imagination and confidence to pursue major goals and the will power to resist the temptations of pursuing superficial activities.

8 Dealing with Uncertainty - a deep and specialized understanding or meta-wisdom that creates a decision making system built around the developing the best approach to problem solving. This demands being adaptive and knowing when to break from tradition and flawed habits. There must be willingness to change. This requires having the cognitive flexibility and awareness to gain new information sources that affirm best decision making practices.

The philosophers revered by Western civilization valued knowledge and wisdom. Socrates, for instance, would often use an intense and sometimes brutal questioning style. As J. Miller points out in *Examined Lives: From Socrates to Nietzsche,* Socrates believed that false confidence was a major barrier to wisdom and used relentless cross-examining to remind people of their limited knowledge. Basically, the wise are aware of how much they do not

> In general, the Socratic method encourages people to become aware of the limitations of their knowledge and recognize the need to study more and seek advice from others.

know, and it is common for those who are wise to frequently point out what they do not know. (Consider, for example, interviews with the Dalai Lama, Mahatmas Gandhi, and Nelson Mandela.) In contrast, those lacking wisdom may work from a foundation of flawed assumption and a false sense of confidence that may lead them to making poor choices. Those who pursue wisdom are dedicated to learning because knowledge helps them in making decisions and enhances their understanding of complex problems, as well as from a love of knowledge for its own sake. Of course, wisdom fosters creative solutions to problems. Those who possess wisdom often become indispensable to their colleagues, families, and organizations.

Socrates recognized, of course, the limits of personal knowledge. As N. Haynes and P. Phillips have pointed out, he would ask colleagues questions as a way to help them learn how to monitor their biased thinking, correct flawed definitions of ideas (e.g. romantic love versus maternal love), and examine information more fully. In general, the Socratic method encourages people to become aware of the limitations of their knowledge and recognize the need to study more and seek advice from others.

During my journey through eight degree programs, I became aware that the brightest students did not always graduate. Intelligence does not guarantee success. Being teachable, learning to ask relevant questions, and being willing to ask for help are important when seeking to achieve positive results. There were students with a false sense of confidence who relied on study methods and knowledge that had worked for them in the past. Teachers in my graduate history program expected students to have a good working knowledge of history, to keep up with the latest scholarship, and to demonstrate their insights in the challenging essay tests and numerous term papers that were assigned. Sadly, some of the brightest students struggled with the academic expectations.

When asked for help, I was glad to share my process. My study approach was to rewrite all lectures into my own words, thoroughly read the assigned materials, read literature beyond the required assignments, create potential essay questions, and practice writing responses to those questions. The study routine gave me a sense of personal ownership of the subject matter and prepared me for the comprehensive written and oral exams that came later in my graduate work.

Creating

2 *Encouraging Creativity*

> "It may be that those who do most dream most."
>
> STEPHEN LEACOCK

Researchers have often written about how American teachers have not made student creativity a priority in their instructional plans and goals. In fact, studies such as Howard B. Parkhurst's have repeatedly shown how schooling experiences stifle or suppress the students' imaginations and individuals become more cautious and less willing to take intellectual risks. Grading has a strong focus on rewarding students for error-free work and punishing students for their mistakes. The grading system often has a strong performance emphasis that misses the importance of learning through exploration and making mistakes. A study by Schacter, Thum, and Zifkin found that teachers who integrate creativity into their daily lessons had a positive impact on student learning. Students displayed a major increase in their academic achievement when they had more opportunities to develop problem-solving skills. This has important implications in an era of high-stakes, standardized testing.

Defining the term *creativity* can be elusive; perhaps writers do not want to diminish the positive connotations associated with the word. James Kaufman and Robert Sternberg defined creativity as having three elements: "first, those ideas must represent something different, new, or innovative. Second, they need to be of high quality. Third, creative ideas must also be appropriate to the task at hand. Thus, a creative response to a problem is a new, good, and relevant." Ronald Beghetto shares a contemporary definition of creativity that stresses the capacity to produce novel (original/unexpected) work. This understanding will establish boundaries for originality and helps individuals identify whether a product or idea is creative.

The history of creativity involves briefly reviewing several major developments during the past sixty years. Reviewing creativity definitions reveals how the term contains intriguing qualities that are sometimes difficult to explain concisely. Researchers began using three primary ways to study creativity: personality variables, motivational variables and sociocultural environment. Carl Rogers and Abraham Maslow represent leaders in the humanistic psychology who promoted the idea of self-actualization arising through a combination of self-acceptance and a supportive environment. In contrast to the humanistic approach, the 1950s-1970s era witnessed the growth of new creative tests.

The tests were designed to provide a better understanding of human achievement and abilities beyond the intelligence tests. Identifying the gifted and talented would help teachers provide assistance to those who could use their creativity in future careers in science and technology. J. P. Guilford and E. P. Torrance were leading psychologists, and their studies and publications led to defining creativity with the terms *fluency*, *flexibility*, and *originality*. The terms reflect characteristics of creative people which can vary between individuals. Guilford's Structure of the Intellect Model contained over 120 traits and 24 traits associated with divergent thinking. Torrance investigated gifted children and developed

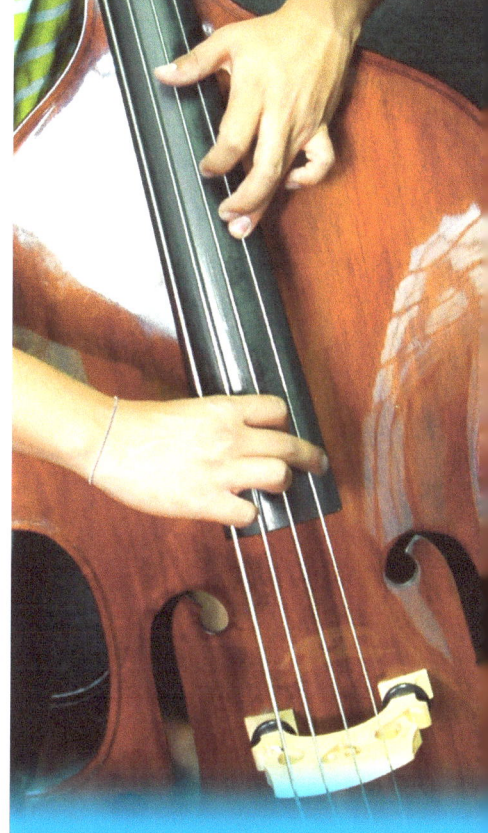

the Torrance Tests of Creative Thinking, which evolved from Guilford's model and measured divergent thinking. During the 1960s, schools implemented educational programs designed to teach critical thinking, but there is a lack of evidence whether the programs increased creative skills. Researchers studied characteristics associated with creativity, such as having a strong work ethic and being dedicated and determined to work through difficulties to complete tasks. Personality tests failed to accurately identify exceptional talent or creative traits in children. The tests were better at identifying social achievement than measuring creativity.

Keith Sawyer in *Explaining Creativity: The Science of Human Innovation* observes that cognitive psychologists in the 1970s gave greater attention to mental processes and less the concept of creative personalities. The research change did create new developments. Cognitive studies had supported the idealist theory that once a creative idea or concept was produced, it was not crucial to apply the idea. Creative studies have demonstrated flaws in the idealist theory. In contrast, action theory advocates the execution of ideas. Creativity happens over time because of the need to experiment, explore, and test ideas.

Teresa Amiable, who heads the Entrepreneurial Management Unit at

> Creativity happens over time because of the need to experiment, explore and test ideas.

Harvard University, was a pioneer in using socio-psychological factors during the 1980s. The componential model consists of domain-relevant skills which involve technical and knowledge skills. A portion of these skills are innate, and others are acquired through informal and formal education. A second set of skills transcends any specific domain and includes any place where the individual is seeking to be innovative.

Creative-relevant skills use the strategy known as breaking set while problem solving. The person leaves an ineffective problem approach and uses heuristic knowledge to produce novel ideas. A common misconception is the need to break from the past to be creative. Rather, creativity builds on past experiences. Also, the individual's attitude plays a key role in problem-solving situations. Those who are intrinsically motivated will increase the probability of being able to successfully generate a creative response. Artists, writers, and scientists are known for being passionate about their endeavors. Therefore, the creative person has established a vital connection between passion and motivation that fuels original thinking and productive results.

The 1990s witnessed efforts to explain the multidimensional nature of creativity. Lubart and Sternberg's investment theory takes an economic perspective, arguing that people will buy low and sell high. Buying low is devoting attention to unpopular ideas because of their potential. The individual will study and promote new ideas even when others fail to support them. The ideas will become more popular due to the creative thinker's determination and skill at persuading others to value and accept the unique ideas. Then, as the ideas become popular, the creative thinker will sell high. Next, the person will leave the popular idea and start investigating a new unpopular idea. The creativity economic explanation does offer insights into those who take a novel approach to problem solving.

Research studies have identified important elements of sustaining creativity. One good approach is found in Robert Weisburg's book *Creativity: Understanding Innovation in Problem Solving, Science, Invention, and the Arts:*

① Intellectual abilities - ability to develop a unique problem perspective beyond the ordinary, identify ideas worth studying & ability to convince others to value new ideas

② Domain knowledge - ability to use information to produce new ideas

③ Independent personality - autonomy of thought, essential when advocating unpopular ideas

④ Supportive setting - original thought is reinforced and rewarded

The list reflects how promoting original thinking requires developing cognitive skills, subject-knowledge expertise, independent thinking, and having a supportive environment for novel ideas. Creative people are effective at being problem finders, noticing what others miss. They cultivate the ability to filter and select relevant ideas to solve problems. Researchers continue to study the cognitive skills associated with problem finding. The modern emphasis on spontaneity has neglected the role of problem selection and preparation. For instance, Impressionist painters in Europe were trained in academies where detailed planning was required, such as selecting the appropriate historical or mythical theme. Painting would begin only after extensive experimenting with colors and making preliminary sketches. This highlights the need for more research into understanding the influences of social and cultural factors (e.g. individualism) on stimulating originality.

The creative person has a flexible mental attitude with openness to considering alternative ideas and solutions. Writers affirm the work of early researchers by stressing the importance of hard work in fostering innovative ideas (e.g. Halpern & Sawyer). A good work ethic enables individuals to have the patience and determination essential to producing solutions. Michael Howe's *Genius Explained* stresses that even those considered to be a genius had an exceptional work ethic. Mozart, for example, began performing at European concerts at the age of six and

> Creative teaching reflects teachers who are able to use their imagination to devise engaging and interesting approaches to learning the subject matter.

composed symphonies when he was nine years old. In 1786, one of his most famous successful musical works was *The Marriage of Figaro*.

Teaching creatively is vital to the learning process. Students need to learn how to develop original thinking and problem-solving skills that are essential in personal and professional settings. Creative exercises make learning relevant and foster an environment that promotes a life-long love for knowledge. Students should be encouraged to channel their emotional energies into their daily educational experiences.

Creative teaching reflects teachers who are able to use their imagination to devise engaging and interesting approaches to learning the subject matter. Educators can help by identifying abilities and encouraging people to express novel ideas and produce original work. Creative teaching represents a vital part of best practices. According to Wayne Morris "all the characteristics of good teaching—including high motivation, high expectations, the ability to communicate and listen and the ability to interest, engage and inspire."

Creativity research affirms the importance being teachable and open to new ideas and experiences. Perhaps a reason our schools, religious groups, business companies, and government agencies struggle is due to having a rigid and conforming culture. Best practices do not arise out of a vacuum but must be supported by a culture that encourages people to experiment with innovative ideas and products. Original thinking and novel ideas should be affirmed and honored.

Robert Sternberg's *College Admissions for the 21st Century* encourages educators to promote creativity by helping "students learn to take sensible risks, adults can encourage them to take intellectual risks with courses, with activities, and with what they say to adults—to develop a sense of how to assess risks."

3 *Creativity Challenges in Education*

The histories of creativity and education are linked with early childhood education and in gifted programs. Contemporary American educators work under the directives of the 2001 federal law known as No Child Left Behind. This federal mandate stresses measuring student achievement through high-stakes testing for all public schools in America. The schools that have chronic low test scores are subject to dramatic government action, such as firing teachers and principals or having the school governed by a private firm or the state department of education. A strong focus on testing and standards has fostered a narrower educational perspective on knowledge and learning. Educators strive to meet short-term student achievement goals that have been established

> "Everyone is capable of being creative, no matter your profession or your specific talents and interests."
>
> J. PINCOTT

by the government. School administrators and teachers are rewarded for quickly improving test scores. Sadly, test scores are the ultimate criteria for measuring school success.

Matthew Makel, a gifted education researcher, says "a fifth-grade teacher is not rewarded when students who had been in her class grow up to be creative thinkers or civic-minded citizens. However, her principal is likely to point out if her current students are not performing well on state standardized tests." A growing number of American schools are linking teacher salaries to student test scores. This creates another barrier to integrating creativity into their classrooms. There are concerns that testing expectations will cause teachers to favor knowledge recall over understanding and basic competence skills above pursuing unique ideas.

Teachers are concerned by the trend of schools using more rigid curriculum materials containing instructor scripts, lesson plans, textbooks, and tests carefully aligned to standardized tests. The approach reflects a scientific management or business model that undermines teacher autonomy and professional expertise. Barry Shwartz and Kenneth Sharpe's *Practical Wisdom: The Right Way to Do the Right Thing* observes that "one of the chief criticisms many teachers make is that the system is dumbing down their teaching. It is de-skilling them." Today's educational reformers fail to address the need for students to enjoy the learning process. The debate over classroom work reflects competing visions of what constitutes a good education.

As a veteran educator, I find it tragic to watch bright, energetic youth become lethargic about education. Perhaps the real problem lies with adults who lack a comprehensive view of learning, adults who are guilty

of classifying real learning as being a difficult and frustrating experience. And the emphasis on testing in public schools is part of the source of this problem, reflecting as it does a narrow and rigid perspective regarding the teaching and learning process.

The focus on preparing for and taking tests is creating a generation of students who equate learning with test results. John Taylor Gatto's *Weapons of Mass Instruction: A School Teacher's Journey Through the Dark World of Compulsory Schooling* criticizes American public schools, saying that the system is "deliberately designed to produce mediocre intellects, to hamstring the inner life, to deny students appreciable leadership skills, and to ensure docile and incomplete citizens — all in order to render the populace 'manageable.'"

Of course, there are educators who are striving to foster critical and creative thinking in their classrooms, but their efforts are not consistently supported by their schools. Much too often, it seems to me, the main focus is the transmission of knowledge for testing. This educational approach diminishes opportunities for students to learn about how to acquire and apply wisdom in their daily lives.

Researchers continue to explore why the message and importance of creativity has been lost. One clue is the finding that teachers are ambivalent about valuing creativity while trying to cover subject content and prepare students for tests. Robert Sternberg and other researchers have found that teacher-centered lessons arise more often because they are an effective way to review information and check the student's recall of factual information. The increased investment of time devoted to students using lower cognitive skills places a greater stress on memory

> The emphasis on testing in public schools reflects a narrow and rigid perspective on the teaching and learning process.

and analytical skills while neglecting the development of creative problem-solving skills. Teachers can suppress creative student expression by moving quickly through the material and controlling class dialogs, dismissing any unexpected novel or unique student ideas. This practice is justified to a degree, considering the subject content that must be taught and larger class sizes.

Yet, there is a real educational cost to teachers dismissing unique thoughts. Ronald Beghetto notes that "though they allow the teacher to move ahead with the lesson as planned, and do not appear punitive, they give students a clear message that some ideas won't be talked about, even if they seem relevant and important to students." Although educators sometimes struggle in their handling of original student-discussion comments, many do appreciate the benefits of creativity. I have noticed how students learn how to generate a diversity of ideas, gain new insights into problems, and make meaningful knowledge connections.

Accountability and high-stakes tests have become part of today's American schools, impacting the entire educational system. Classes have become more test-centered as teachers strive to cover the subject content. Moving quickly through the curriculum reflects an emphasis on efficiency, but can result in the loss of important learning opportunities for both students and instructors. When teachers develop a learning environment that allows student responses to vary in creating the correct answer, students may begin to feel "surprised, puzzled, excited, and comfortable with being wrong (Makel)." While teaching classes, it has become apparent to me that reflective discussions enable students to acquire a deeper understanding of the subject matter, gain confidence by having their ideas valued in a public forum, and promotes creative problem-solving attitudes.

Teachers can assist their students in becoming more sophisticated in their understanding of creativity. James Kaufman and Ronald Beghetto have developed a model that offers four categories:

1. **Big C:** these are legendary creativity (e.g. Mozart, Gandhi or Dickinson), eminent creative contributions (e.g. Winston Churchill) and winners of a Pulitzer Prize (e.g. Ann Taylor)

2. **Pro-C:** professional creativity (e.g. jazz musician)

3. **Mini-C:** personal and developmental creativity, dynamic process of building personal knowledge

4. **Little-C:** inherent in the learning process (e.g. creative insights)

Kaufman and Beghetto's model promotes recognizing different types of creativity and supports the principle that every student can be creative and that creativity is not restricted to certain backgrounds or personality characteristics. This helps avoid the tendency to dwell mainly on well-known individuals—Albert Einstein, for instance—that can minimize the importance of recognizing everyday originality.

Teachers can devote time to test preparation and integrate creativity into their classes. One example is an excellent language exercise by David Levy from his book *Tools of Critical Thinking: Metathoughts for Psychology*. Levy had designed a list of forty negative terms for person A. The student must create new and more positive terms for person B. Students are given examples such as "if person A is greedy, then Person B is assertive." I have has used the vocabulary exercise in undergraduate university classes and have found it to be an effective way to spark the student's imaginative and creative selection of words. Students have produced unique and sometimes funny terms that make the exercise enjoyable.

Invented situations (often based on actual events) or scenarios can help teachers guide students in developing reflective thinking skills and understanding, for example, that sometimes ethical dilemmas require novel solutions. For instance, teachers could share a situation where a university instructor has lied on his or her résumé and managed to secure a teaching position even though the person did not have the required college degrees. The individual worked for twenty years before university officials discovered the lie. After being introduced to the scenario, they can be challenged to act as a university administrator and develop a solution for the ethical problem.

According to one study, the seven traits of creative people are "independence of judgment, self-confidence, attraction to complexity, aesthetic orientation, openness to experience, risk taking, and self-actualization" (Sternberg, Lubart, Kaufman & Pretz). Clearly, these traits can be important factors in the development of an educated person. The development of creativity can become a vibrant part of the curriculum and reinforce critical-thinking skills. Teachers can use exercises such as the two noted above to help students develop problem-solving skills, such as learning to sort through ideas to identify the important ones, as well as to further develop other important characteristics. Educators can enhance their creativity resources by reading literature on the subject, identifying practical illustrations, and sharing ideas with colleagues through learning communities.

> The development of creativity can become a vibrant part of the curriculum and reinforce critical thinking skills.

4 *Improving Creativity*

Educators wonder about how to improve their student's creativity to solve complex problems and produce unique products. Cognitive psychologists have recognized an important paradox involving playfulness and discipline found in creative accomplishments. Creative individuals have a level of persistence that is rarely matched by others. The determination gives them the endurance to handle adversity and solve difficult problems. They often possess playful attitudes that enable them to freely explore ideas, providing a definite break from seriously pondering complex ideas and fostering a receptive mental outlook for considering novel concepts or ideas.

> "If the next generation is to face the future with zest and self-confidence, we must educate them to be original as well as competent."
>
> MIHALY CSIKSZENTMIHALYI

Educators need to provide opportunities that foster original thinking and may help students produce novel products. For instance, interactive computer puzzles and knowledge-oriented games are more playful and represent a change in daily learning routines. Student curiosity should be continually encouraged by developing a learning climate that stimulates risk taking and exploration of ideas. Perhaps students appear to be bored in class because the work is devoid of intellectual challenge and fails to spark their imaginations!

Learning to tap into creativity must begin with understanding the nature of this unique character trait. Robert Harris has developed a description of creativity that stresses the need for hard work and a flexible mental attitude:

An Ability: A simple definition is that creativity is the ability to imagine or invent something new.

An Attitude: Creativity is also an attitude: the attitude to accept change and newness, a willingness to play with ideas and possibilities, a flexibility of outlook, the habit of enjoying the good, while looking for ways to improve it.

A Process: Creative people work hard and continually to improve ideas and solutions, by making gradual alternations and refinements to their works.

Michael Howe has conducted a biographical analysis of people who were considered to be geniuses because of their exceptional work, Thomas Edison, for example. Howe's examination of their lives demonstrates that most had an outstanding work ethic. They were diligent and patient and skilled in the use of problem-solving techniques that gave them a process for seeking solutions.

Motivation plays a major role in people being creative. Extrinsic motivational techniques can be financial incentives in the business world; grades serve as an incentive for students. Yet, these can have a limited influence on individual performance. In contrast, intrinsic motivation to do various tasks can reflect a passion or strong interest, something an individual enjoys doing. A major criticism of contemporary education is the emphasis on curriculum conformity, beginning in early schooling experiences and continuing even through higher-education course work.

Teachers can inspire intrinsic motivation. I have taken Teresa Amabile's six strategies and applied them to an educational setting to highlight several of the ways these strategies can have a positive impact on intrinsic motivation:

1 challenge - creating learning activities that stretch but do not overwhelm the student. The individual should be effectively tested beyond their current knowledge and skills.

2 freedom - instructor can enhance reflective skills by having clearly defined goals that give students the opportunity to complete an assignment in a variety of ways that foster self-directed learning.

3 resources - this can involve having access to online libraries and the quality of interpersonal relationships between students and between students and their instructors.

4 work-group features - learning situations for teams that include use of a diversity of cognitive skills and professional, cultural, and educational experiences can enhance creativity.

5 supervisory encouragement - teachers play a vital role in helping students work through anxiety when tackling difficult assignments. Professional judgment is needed to know when to give more detailed instructions to students who are struggling because part of the process is learning to be patient when working through complex problem-solving issues. Students who lack confidence in their learning skills or fear failure can be encouraged by allowing them to make mistakes and experience the joys of being successful in their work.

6 organizational support - teachers and students need to feel that their work is important. Teachers can become discouraged about integrating innovative methods into their classes if the work is rarely affirmed by their leaders.

So, educators need to examine whether their teaching practices are encouraging original thinking or making learning a mechanical exercise. Perhaps it is time to consider new approaches that engage the student's hearts and minds and stimulate novel thoughts and ideas. Amabile conducted a research project on creativity that offers help for devising such new approaches. Amabile's team collected information from 238 individuals involving almost 12,000 daily journals of notes on work experiences. The comments reflect the ideas and thoughts of those working on projects from seven different companies. Bill Breen has pointed out that Amabile's research study has identified six myths about creativity:

1. **Creativity comes from creative types:** Creativity depends upon a number of things: experience, including knowledge and technical skills; talent; an ability to think in new ways; and the capacity to push through uncreative dry spells.

2. **Money is a creativity motivator:** People are most creative when they care about their work and they're stretching their skills.

3. **Time pressure fuels creativity:** Time pressure stifles creativity because people can't deeply engage with the problem.

4. **Fear forces breakthroughs:** We found that creativity is positively associated with joy and love and negatively with anger, fear, and anxiety.

5. **Competition beats collaboration:** In our surveys we found that creativity takes a hit when people in a group compete instead of collaborate.

6. **A streamlined organization is a creative organization:** Creativity suffers greatly during downsizing. Every single one of the stimulants to creativity in the work environment went down significantly during downsizing.

There are misconceptions about how to motivate people to be more productive. Tragically, some leaders rely upon fear as a way to control and manipulate people. Insecure leaders can send mixed messages, which can cause people to doubt their talents and skills. Individuals in negative work settings must develop short- and long-term career goals. Creativity can flourish in the midst of adverse circumstances. I once was in a graduate school class that had a total lack of communication and no teacher feedback on assignments for the entire course. The negative experience prompted me to develop a research on study of interactivity (communication, feedback and participation) in online graduate classes. I created a research project that help launch a new career as a distance educator for me.

There is wisdom in carefully assessing negative past events and viewing them as learning opportunities. Educators can use narratives from history or literature about how others have used wisdom to overcome obstacles to reach their dreams and goals. For instance, Alexander Dumas' book *The Count of Monte Cristo* is an inspirational story on the wisdom of forgiveness. Stories help students reflect on the importance of making wise choices. Meaningful stories will be recalled long after the class has ended and can have enduring influence.

> Stories help students reflect on the importance of making wise choices.

5 *Becoming Indispensable*

In the 21st century, the American economic crisis has created chaos, affecting millions of people who have suffered the loss of jobs and homes. Unemployment continues to be a major social problem as individuals try to figure out ways to find work. Most political and business experts offer little hope and wisdom during these difficult times. In contrast, Seth Godin in his book *Linchpin: Are You Indispensable?* offers practical advice to those who want to better utilize their talents and skills and work towards increasing their economic security. The first step requires self-reflection and involves answering a series of personal questions:

> "Paint a masterpiece daily. Always autograph your work with excellence."
>
> GREG HICKMAN

1. Do I enjoy my present job? If not, ask what are the reasons for this situation?

2. Does my current work undervalue my talents and abilities?

3. If I am afraid to make changes to my work and life, how can I overcome these fears?

4. What are the type of activities that motivate me and affirm my passion?

5. What are ways that I can start making a difference and become indispensable?

The questions provide a starting point for developing plans for becoming indispensable within an organization or by creating a new job by taking initiative and being creative.

Why do we keep making the same mistakes? Individuals will excessively use their credit cards even though their consistent failures to pay for their purchases by only paying minimum balances will harm their credit. People will reject basic financial advice regarding diversifying their investments and placing their resources into real estate or individual stocks. Then, they witness a severe drop in value of their investments and endure painful financial losses. Perhaps, part of the problem involves a failure to analyze the root cause of our mistakes. Joseph Hallinan says, "We learn so little from experience because we often blame the wrong cause."

I have created a practical list of ten reasons why people fail. It is not a comprehensive list but reflects a variety of ways people can experience negative results.

Fear - afraid to make changes, fearful about new jobs, anxious about whether people might rejection their ideas and plans, economic fears about working independently.

Failure to plan - absence of goals, lack of focus, not willing to experiment to discover passion and talents.

Failure to act - diminished risk taking, lacks initiative, involved in nonproductive activities.

Complacent attitudes - resists making changes, establishes a pattern of low expectations, exhibits negative perspectives on life, is inflexible, demonstrates victim mentality.

Weak people skills - tendency to blame others, not involved in helping others, weak commitments in personal and professional relationships.

Lacks patience - inability to pursue difficult or major goals, unrealistic expectations about the amount of time it takes to succeed, lack of personal discipline, inadequate work ethic.

Dwells on the past - focus on negative memories of past failures and mistakes, inability to forgive oneself or others, relies heavily upon talent but neglects improving abilities.

Resists advice - rejects advice to improve job performance and career opportunities, eliminates or restricts relationships with those who challenge their thinking, plans and ideas.

Indifferent - lacks genuine concern for the welfare of others, selfish, arrogant, greedy, jealous.

Ethical weaknesses - rationalizes poor moral decisions, excessively focused on material possessions, disregard for company and social norms.

My list highlights ways that people can make poor choices and develop negative attitudes and habits. People need to remind themselves that they are a product of their choices and they can take control of their lives. A worthy goal would be to strive to be indispensable, as Godin suggests, which would dramatically change their daily lives. The pursuit of this objective offers opportunities to make important changes in priorities such as identifying *wasted time* and being more productive. There is an assortment of ways to becoming indispensable for those willing to use their imagination and take on new challenges. For instance, individuals need to evaluate their strengths and skills and identify ways to bolster those that may help them reach their goals. The following list reflects my suggestions on how to foster growth, find meaningful work, and secure economic security:

❶ Create goals • establish short- and long-term goals • share objectives to enhance accountability • measure progress • celebrate achievements.

❷ Seek professional growth • identify ways to update skills and knowledge • implement a plan.

❸ Maintain a positive attitude • cultivate a positive perspective toward life and work.

❹ Be creative • develop the habit of being an original thinker • be passionate about ideas • translate thoughts into creative products.

❺ Network • offer valuable insights during conversations • foster productive relationships.

❻ Practice caring communication • show genuine interest in others • seek to brighten the day • personalize interactions • send clear messages • help others feel good about themselves.

❼ Share • pursue opportunities to teach and communicate ideas • strive to become known as a generous person.

❽ Be self-motivated • take initiative and create value for others and their organizations • promote change • inspire greatness in others.

❾ Become a lifelong learner • read and study • become known for having strong intellectual interests.

❿ Pursue excellence • be determined and dedicated to produce quality work • be a person of integrity.

It is interesting that those who are truly interested in becoming indispensable will be proactive and consistently seek new ways to grow and improve. The ten principles above offer a practical and multidimensional approach for pursuing a more meaningful life. It is interesting that the idea of being happy or happiness is connected closely with having positive emotions and being engaged in purposeful work. Happiness is the indirect by-product of living an authentic life.

6 *Talent Alone is Never Enough*

Reality television is interesting to watch. Many so-called reality shows have *experts* that evaluate competitions focused on food, acting, dance, and singing, to name a few topics. People are often too quick to use the term *expert* which has diminished the original intent of the word. Cognitive psychologists stress that it often takes ten years for a person to become an expert in a specific field (Anderson & Schacter). Research studies have found that skill development and developing expertise were tied closely to the quality and quantity of the deliberate practice. (Mentors, too, played a vital role to the learner by providing guidance, monitoring progress and establishing appropriate goals that would promote optimal growth.) Deliberate practice can help less-talented people surpass the achievements of those who are more talented.

Studies of skill acquisition among young athletes, mathematicians, and musicians indicates that individuals followed a similar learning process. In Geoff Colvin's

> "Keep away from people who try to belittle your ambitions. Small people always do that, but the really great make you feel that you, too, can become great."
>
> MARK TWAIN

Talent is Overrated, he stresses the importance of having appropriate guidance, establishing goals, monitoring progress, and having intentional practices that cultivate superior performance. Guided practice is a powerful concept because it demands being teachable, personal discipline, and the willingness to devote countless hours to mastering skills. Superior performance, innovation, and expertise are rewards for those willing to sacrifice for great achievement.

Students and teaching colleagues will frequently ask me questions about completing eight academic degrees. I struggled with how to answer the questions because it is difficult to provide a concise response. I usually just say, *it is who I am*. Each of us is a product of daily choices. During the past thirty years, I have studied eight to ten hours a day, worked full time jobs, and helped raise a family. The studying enabled me to acquire knowledge about a diversity of subjects: sociology, theology, history, cognitive psychology, leadership, philosophy, communication, and education. People will sometimes ask if the constant studying over the years has caused me to miss out on fun activities. There is joy in pursuing one's passion, and mine is teaching, researching, and writing for publication. Yes, there is an element of sacrifice in every worthy endeavor.

Working toward difficult goals demands staying focused and a willingness to work hard on a regular basis for extended periods of time. Academic study is solitary activity

> Working toward difficult goals demands staying focused and a willingness to work hard on a regular basis for extended periods of time.

because of the reading, investigating resources, and writing papers. The solitude offers a wonderful opportunity to cultivate a rich inner life and gain a deeper appreciation for life.

7 *Resiliency*

Each day is filled with an assortment of new challenges, such as paying bills, doctor visits, emailing friends, car repairs, and taking the children to school. The loss of a job represents a unique life event that affects people in a variety of ways. Pride can cause individuals to respond negatively to their job loss. There are stories of men who could not tell their wives about losing their job. Instead, they would leave home each day and drive around the city. During the Great Depression in the 1930s, some men would wear a suit every day, even though they did not have a job. There have been research studies into how people successfully coped with major job issues.

Maddi and Khoshaba conducted a 12 year study of 450 supervisors, managers, and decision makers at Illinois Bell Telephone (IBT). The era involved major changes in the telecommunications industry. During the sixth year of the research project, telephone companies were changed from federally controlled monopolies to deregulated, competitive businesses. In 1982, IBT went from 26,000 employees to 14,000. The deregulation of AT&T and other telephone companies created similarly significant personnel changes. IBT workers

> "What lies behind us and what lies ahead of us are tiny matters compared to what lives within us."
>
> HENRY DAVID THOREAU

> The essence of resiliency is hardiness and the ability to bounce back to foster creative responses to difficult problems.

experienced a diversity of challenges such as having ten different supervisors within a year.

The IBT employees who were resilient faced the stress of their changes by looking at the situation from a broader perspective. People realized that others were struggling, and it was important to take the time to have a deeper understanding of their circumstances. They formed support groups and discussed how to be proactive and encourage each other. Directly facing major changes enabled people to cultivate trust and foster positive attitudes. Resilient employees learned to develop constructive relationships that effectively resolved conflicts and encouraged win-win solutions. Individuals viewed problems as opportunities to strengthen their work relationships. People worked hard to preserve bridges to others that were strong during difficult times, and these relationships were considered vital to their growth. The transformational ability and social support enabled individuals to translate adversity into opportunities for growth. Maddi and Khoshaba identified four traits in those who demonstrated exceptional coping skills: thrives on change, takes decisive action, resilient with family, and future oriented.

Resiliency is a wonderful character trait that enables people to make positive contributions in their relationships with colleagues and family members. The essence of resiliency is hardiness and the ability to bounce back to foster creative responses to difficult problems. There is no substitute for endurance and determination to pursue difficult and challenging goals. They require cultivating the ability to adapt to changing circumstances and staying focused to work diligently even when the ultimate goal appears remote. Resiliency equips individuals to make wise choices by striving for excellence while others fall to the alluring temptation to take short cuts and settle for less in their lives.

8   Helping Others

Selfishness is a deadly sin because the selfish person is absorbed in meeting his or her own needs and disregards others. Those who are consumed with promoting and protecting their own interests can quickly become selfish individuals who can cause emotional pain, discouragement, and loss of self-esteem. Prolonged selfish behavior can lead to martial conflicts, affairs, job issues, and divorces.

There are many ways that selfishness can appear. During my undergraduate days at the University of Northern Iowa, I would have friends visit me who would need a place to stay for a night. One of my college friends had a single dorm room with two beds. Yet, every time she was asked to share her room with one of my female friends, she always refused.

> "The real test of character for a leader is to nurture those people whose stars may shine as brightly as— or even brighter than— the leader's own."
>
> WARREN BENNIS

I met her several years later at a doctor's office. She chatted quietly for awhile and revealed her guilt over being so selfish about not sharing the dorm room with others. The confession surprised me. Then, she started

34   WISDOM: *Making Good Choices with Imperfect Knowledge*

to walk away from me, I was stunned by the next comment, "I have cancer." She walked swiftly to her car and left. The brief encounter made wonder whether the cancer had made this individual more reflective about her life. Hopefully, it will not take a serious illness or death of a colleague or spouse to remind us of the need to help and love others.

Today's writers have explored various social issues relating to young adults, such as binge drinking and drug use. The emphasis on negative social trends and attitudes of Jean M. Twenge and W. Keith Campbell's *The Narcissism Epidemic: Living in the Age of Entitlement* has generated critical reactions from those within the academic community. Young adults are criticized for their self-admiration and being selfish due the prevalence of social networking sites built upon an egocentric focus. The mass media through advertising, television shows, music videos, and films often do portray instant gratification as a positive social behavior and emphasize the wonders of fame and celebrity status.

According to Robert C. Roberts and W. Jay Wood "generosity is a disposition to give valuable things—material goods, time, attention, energy, credit, the benefit of a doubt, knowledge—to other persons." Generosity is related to the idea of freedom and the desire for the best for the other and fulfillment. Those who freely share with others will provide appropriate gifts to for the recipient. The stingy and greedy individuals suffer from bondage.

Stingy persons are anxious and fearful about losing what they consider to be valuable, their possessions, for example. Greedy attitudes involve perceived threats from competition or being open to potential

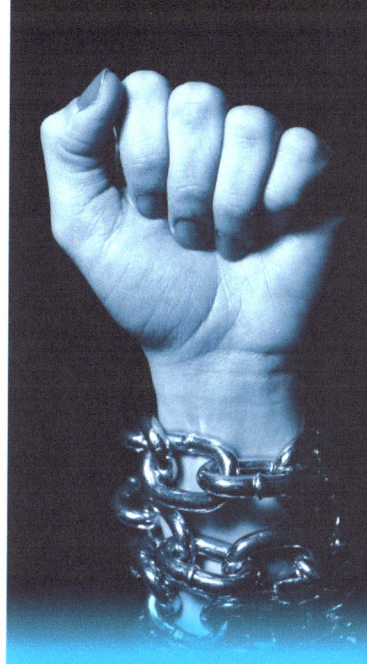

The stingy and greedy individuals suffer from bondage.

disappointment about winning. The greedy suffer from envy while the stingy face continual anxiety.

In contrast, generous people experience freedom from these negative vices and are able to wisely manage their disappointments with emotional maturity. People will sometimes say, "I will never trust anyone." Yet, trust is the foundation for personal and professional relationships. Those who are generous handle personal frustrations by seeking to learn from those experiences and develop greater discernment about human relationships.

The changes in American culture are complex, multidimensional, and are difficult to analyze within the framework of narcissistic explanation. Yet, even casual daily public observations will affirm a growing trend toward people being rude while driving or shopping. One wonders how much of a role selfish behavior and attitudes play in divorces and difficult work relationships.

Individuals are the product of their daily choices. John Maxwell talks about individuals who strive to daily invest in the lives of others by taking positive action:

> People are insecure... *give them confidence.*
>
> People want to feel special... *sincerely compliment them.*
>
> People desire a better tomorrow... *show them hope.*
>
> People need to be understood... *listen to them.*
>
> People are selfish... *speak to their needs first.*
>
> People are emotionally low... *encourage them.*
>
> People want to be associated with success... *help them win.*

Maxwell's recommendations are general and must be translated into specific and personal interactions. Making the effort to truly help others is one of the traits of a wise person. Those who have had a positive impact on others often have freely shared their advice and encouragement. The secure leader has the mindset to help others to grow and mature in their skills and knowledge. There is a great need for more mentors who are dedicated to helping others to reach their career goals.

I once helped a student who needed immediate assistance to complete his doctoral degree. The student wanted to quickly complete his dissertation due to having a terminal disease. He wanted the degree to be a legacy for his family. The dissertation committee worked diligently to provide timely feedback to the student and offered advice to speed up the research work. After the student finished his degree program, the individual repeatedly thanked me for helping him. Yet, I was truly blessed by being able to work with him. The individual never complained about his health problems and always had a positive attitude. I will always remember him for his courage.

Thinking about wisdom offers us a new approach to decision making and may provide an opportunity for us to make better choices in our personal and professional lives. The future is, and always has been, unpredictable; the present, too, presents its own uncertainties. For many of us, life has taken on a more fragile tone, even if we are not directly affected by the economic turmoil that is rife today.

As governments suffer the consequences of chronic unemployment problems and public-service systems that lack financial resources, our communities seem less strong. The stresses of the normal passages of life are made more difficult by the sense that the world around us is less sturdy than in the past. As the old paradigms wobble and new ways of functioning on a day-to-day basis, due, in part, to advances in technology, previously useful approaches to making decisions may not serve us as they did in the past.

Reaching

9   *Setting Goals*

The mention of the need to set goals can cause people to respond in a variety of ways. My university students are sometimes hesitant to share their goals with others because of the possibility of not reaching them. There are concerns about being embarrassed in conversations with friends and colleagues if they are asked about a goal that has been elusive to reach. Having worries about what others think about specific goals can be counterproductive if the individual becomes fearful about setting and then acting to achieve possible goals.

> "On the journey to greatness, you are the archer, the arrow, and the target. Draw your bow and take aim on what you want."
>
> — NOAH BENSHEA

Individuals should devote time to evaluating their personal and professional aspirations and dreams by asking questions. For instance, what would I enjoy doing in one or five years from now? What new skills and knowledge do I need? What future job or occupation is worthy of great personal sacrifice?

The Socratic questions help filter diverse ideas about the future and highlight the values and priorities that reflect what is important to you. The planning process enables people to create goals that spark their imagination and energize them to pursue endeavors that make life an adventure. Goals are empowering and offer new opportunities to take control of your life. They fuel hope.

Cognitive psychologists such as Reeve argue that the key to goal creation is establishing a realistic and challenging set of goals that involve both short- and long-term objectives. Goals must be difficult; the difficulty helps energize and motivate us to pursue them. The goals should be specific enough to offer direction and a clear focus. Cognitive psychologists acknowledge that a person's actual performance is influenced by a variety of factors, such as ability, resources, coaching, and training. Having specific and difficult objectives without the additional factors might not improve performance.

> The planning process enables people to create goals that spark their imagination and energizes them to pursue endeavors that make life an adventure.

Choices with Imperfect Knowledge

Most people will become discouraged or quit before experiencing success, limiting their motivation to pursue future goals. Individuals need to devote adequate attention to planning and self-evaluation of their skills and abilities when developing goals.

Establishing short-term goals enables people to have regular feedback to measure their degree of progress. The information will either result in emotional satisfaction or dissatisfaction with the performance. If the feedback affirms that the individual is operating at or above the goal expectations, the individual will probably feel competent to establish new and higher goals. If the feedback is negative, this signals the need to increase the efforts to achieve goal plans. John Marshall Reeve observes that feedback "provides the emotional punch that brings the goal-setting process to life within the experiences of felt satisfaction and felt dissatisfaction."

Reeve also sees that the acceptance or rejection of goals can be influenced by four factors.

1. perceived difficulty of the imposed goal
2. participation in the goal-setting process
3. credibility of the person assigning the goal
4. extrinsic incentives

Accepting a new goal is multifaceted interaction of these four factors. Researchers have found that the highest rate of acceptance of goals involves the perception that the goal is moderately attainable, personally established or negotiated, assigned by a trustworthy colleague, and offers the potential for benefits.

There are definite risks in setting goals due to a failure to reach the objectives. Difficult goals establish performance standards that can generate stress over reaching them. Negative feedback can trigger feelings of being inadequate, a loss of respect among friends or coworkers, and even financial setbacks.

When educators or business leaders implement goals through fear or striving to control personal behavior, there can be a diversity of unintended negative outcomes, such as suppressing creativity and fostering barriers to internal motivation. When imposed goals are placed upon people without their participation in the goal-creation process, the result may be a diminished passion for work due to a weakened sense of autonomy.

Goals should not be too easy to obtain. Setting goals offers an opportunity to create a challenge, to stretch. The primary reason people struggle or even fail to achieve their goals is due to failing to develop an action plan. Establishing specific, goal-oriented steps is essential in overcoming the inevitable challenges that will occur over time. The plan offers a concrete vision and focus to guide one in the midst of daily distractions.

The ability to be persistent about pursuing a goal enables individuals to overcome setbacks. Determination is the "game changer." This positive character trait empowers people to achieve challenging goals and generates the confidence to set new and more demanding goals.

The goal setter's frame of reference is an important consideration. A struggle in creating goals might be due to past negative experiences of setting unrealistic goals. Perhaps, a better alternative is to consider establishing doable, short-term objectives that are challenging but realistic. Then, as you experience success and positive experiences in reaching those goals, you will begin to aim for larger goals — and achieve even greater success.

10 *Encouraging People's Dreams*

The benefit of having a dream is being able to transcend daily circumstances and think of enjoying a better future. Dreams can enable people to have the determination to work diligently for long periods of time at tasks that might be unpleasant but provide necessary financial support. Dreams give people hope for a brighter future: a more meaningful job, new educational or business opportunities, a loving relationship. Never underestimate the power of dreams to sustain a positive attitude in the midst of difficult times. Breaking down the dream into short- and long-term goals can transform the dream into reality. John Maxwell and Les Parrot offer six practical ways to encourage people to seek their dreams:

> "Encouragement is oxygen to the soul."
>
> GEORGE MATTHEW ADAMS

1. **Ask them to share their dream with you.** Everyone has a dream, but few people are asked about it.

2. **Affirm the person as well as the dream.** Let the person know that you not only value his or her dream but that you recognize traits in that individual that can help him or her achieve it.

3. **Ask about the challenges they must overcome to reach their dream.** Few people ask others about their dreams; even fewer try to find out what kinds of hurdles the person is up against to pursue them.

4. **Offer your assistance.** No one achieves a worthwhile dream

alone. You'll be amazed by how people light up when you offer to help them achieve their dream.

⑤ Revisit their dream with them on a consistent basis. If you really want to help others with their dreams, don't make it a one-time activity you mark off your list. Check in with them to see how they're doing and to lend assistance.

⑥ Determine daily to be a dream booster, not a dream buster. Everyone has a dream, and everyone needs encouragement. Set your mental radar to pick up on others' dreams and help them along.

People are at various stages in their pursuit of goals and dreams. A valuable book on identifying a job and career that is meaningful is Nancy Anderson's *Work with Passion: How To Do What You Love for a Living*. It is interesting to observe how people respond to others who have lost a dream. In 1980, the United States was in difficult economic times, and people were buying homes at 18%. My annual income as a campus minister at the University of Northern Iowa was approximately $3,000. Due to unemployment, people were not able to give as much money to churches, adversely affecting my financial situation. I made the tough decision to quit pursuing my dream of being a campus minister. It takes courage to pursue challenging dreams as it does to let go of those dreams. The loss of the dream created a void in my life. During this time, I worked a variety of jobs, such as painting, cleaning school buildings at night, and working with severely handicapped adults. It was not easy to identify a new career after investing heavily in one major goal. Eventually, after almost three years of soul searching, I decided to become a high school teacher. In 1975 while in seminary, the idea of becoming a college teacher became a long term goal of mine.

It is interesting to observe how people respond to others who have lost a dream.

After ten years of teaching high school students and earning three more graduate degrees, my goal of teaching university students became a reality. It wasn't easy, and I did have struggles along the way. However, I can attest to the fact that there is joy in achieving a significant goal and that getting to that goal builds confidence to pursue even more challenging dreams.

11 *Why is it difficult to learn from mistakes?*

Why do we keep making the same mistakes? Individuals will excessively use their credit cards even though the failure to pay for their purchases will harm their credit and could have long term negative consequences. People will reject basic financial advice to diversify their investments and place their resources into real estate or individual stocks. Then, witness the a severe drop in value of their investments and endure painful financial losses. Mistakes are judged by the severity of the consequences Perhaps, part of the problem involves a failure to analysis the root cause of our mistakes. Yet, even experts struggle to correctly identify the source of a major problem.

> "There is no education like adversity."
>
> BENJAMIN DISRAELI

There are definite potential dangers when poor decisions are made by financial advisors or military leaders that could cause the loss of enormous sums of money and even lives. In his book, *Failing Forward: Turning Mistakes into Stepping Stones for Success,* John Maxwell gives ten reasons people experience failure. (The commentary for each reason is mine.)

1. **Poor people skills:** people can try to blame office politics; the real problem has to do with the failure to connect in relationships.

2. **A negative attitude:** those who take a jaded view of life will struggle with being sad or even miserable because they feel trapped by their circumstances.

3. **A bad fit:** being in the wrong job can generate a constant sense of failure due to talents and abilities not being utilized and values not being affirmed.

4. **Lack of focus:** the inability to focus on tasks causes wasted time and resources and hinders people from reaching their goals.

5. **A weak commitment:** the absence of dedication can cause people to give up when they encounter difficulty or failure.

6. **An unwillingness to change:** dwelling on the past and resisting change are deadly habits; inflexibility is the enemy to achievement, growth, and success.

7. **A short-cut mindset:** trying to cut corners is born of impatience and an absence of discipline.

8. **Relying on talent alone:** those who lack a good work ethic will find it difficult to improve and overcome the effects of failures that are a natural and important part of life.

9. **A response to poor information:** the inability to filter information can lead to bad decisions.

10. **No goals:** people who rarely dream about the future will undermine their imagination and ability to formulate goals.

> Sadly, there are those who experience a life filled with regrets about what might have been.

Maxwell's list highlights ways that people can make poor choices or develop negative habits. Sadly, there are those who experience a life filled with regrets about what might have been. Yet, the list is not comprehensive because the reasons for personal failure transcend any neat descriptions and reflect the complexity of human nature.

Those who have constant regret about the past may fail to learn from their mistakes. Negative feelings will keep them from clearly examining their past experiences and undermine their productivity in the present.

Alina Tugend's book *Better by Mistake* discusses the problem of failing to consider the context of past mistakes: "With hindsight bias we tend to think a sequence of events is linear, inevitably leading to one outcome. It causes us to be hard on ourselves and others." Hindsight bias can create a host of emotional and psychological problems. For instance, children who come from divorced homes will sometimes carry guilt about their parents and think of alternative ways they could have helped avoid the divorce. Yet, this type of thinking fails to recognize the fact that the parents are responsible for their own behavior and decisions.

Another negative response to past mistakes is the constant effort to be perfect, to avoid making errors. This is classified as a maladaptive perfectionism. It may undermine, for example, the quality of work. When one is driven by the fear of failure, he or she may delay beginning work and then may avoid having others review and share feedback. Sadly, some people view new projects as another potential way to fail rather than as an opportunity for achievement.

Companies will often try to hide their mistakes to protect their image and competitive position in the marketplace. A major problem is the failure to take personal responsibility and admit mistakes. Individuals will often either hide or justify mistakes, undermining the ability to form a clear picture of what to study and how to correct errors. Paul Schoemaker and Robert Gunther cite four primary reasons people and organizational cultures seek to avoid mistakes or neglect learning from them:

❶ **We are overconfident** - we are often blind to the limits of expertise.

❷ **We are risk averse** - our professional and personal pride is tied up in being right.

❸ **We seek confirming evidence** - because we tend to favor data that support our beliefs, we often don't see the alternatives.

❹ **We assume feedback is reliable** - in examining the validity of intuition, decision researcher Robin Hogarth distinguishes between 'kind' environments, which offer reliable feedback, and 'wicked' ones in which feedback is lacking or misleading. In business, wicked environments are common.

Schoemaker and Gunther's four reasons affirm the importance of taking a fresh perspective on mistakes. There are valuable resources available for studying about this issue, such as Carol Travis and Elliot Arson's *Mistakes Were Made (But Not By Me)* and Sarah Bakewell's *A Life of Montaigne: In One Question and Twenty Attempts at an Answer.* There is wisdom in learning from others through reading books or articles and having conversations with those who are willing to talk about their mistakes.

12 *The Value of Pessimism*

Roger Scruton argues that there is a legitimate place for pessimism in our thinking. He is concerned about an addictive optimism that has arisen and created a dangerous set of illusions. Optimism is destructive because it replaces human reasoning and debate skills. The excessive optimistic perspective rejects efforts to critically examine belief systems and risk factors.

Government leaders who embrace excessively the optimistic mindset are often irresponsible because they will not allow themselves to be held accountable for their beliefs that have created negative social effects (e.g. unemployment). In fact, the political leaders may attack their critics, undermining public debate and having a toxic effect on democratic institutions.

People become disillusioned about how decisions are made when they disregard clear evidence of what might be for the common good. In sharp contrast, Scruton advocates for having more people becoming scrupulous optimists; he uses the example of a female, "one who measures the extent of the problem and consults the existing store of knowledge and authority in order to solve it, relying initiative and inspiration when no other guidance can be found, or some original quirk in her predicament sparks off a matching response in herself."

It is time to seek to truly understand the nature of leadership. There is a tremendous need for genuine leaders who make a positive difference in

> "The wise don't expect to find life worth living; they make it that way."
>
> ANONYMOUS

their businesses, schools, churches, and government. In the book *Your Road Map for Success,* John Maxwell shares ten traits of successful leaders that I have translated into reflective insights:

1. Choose a life dedicated to growth.
2. Make a deliberate choice to start growing today.
3. Strive to be teachable.
4. Focus on developing your potential.
5. Have a healthy dissatisfaction with current accomplishments.
6. Be a lifelong learner.
7. Live a life that is focused on a few major themes.
8. Develop a growth plan to meet short- and long-term goals.
9. Be willing to pay the price for taking risks and making changes in your life.
10. Apply what you have learned and inspire others to become successful leaders.

During my life, my most stressful experiences have been working with insecure and unethical leaders. When I was a teacher in a public high school, I saw that some administrators operated with various agendas that violated professional ethics. They forced out teachers or assistant administrators from their schools. One principal drove out sixty teachers from the high school in two years and tried to make my life miserable.

High school teaching has turned out to be the most difficult job in my career. The school environments were often focused on social and intellectual conformity. Schools are mirroring business models which place a strong emphasis on accountability and efficiency. High-stakes

Schools are mirroring business models with a strong emphasis on accountability and efficiency.

testing tied to a rigid curriculum is discouraging teachers from using their creative teaching skills to meet student needs. In fact, one of the more remarkable incidents in my high school involved a drama teacher who was evaluated and failed because of being too *creative* in her lesson plans! Apparently her classroom activities did not closely follow the state-mandated guidelines and were too open-ended for the evaluator.

Weak educational leaders created a great deal of stress during my high school teaching. A major way of coping for me was to get involved in completing two doctoral degrees and a master's degree. The degree programs were challenging and helped me to be positive and focused on growing and eventually made possible my teaching career in higher education.

13 *Dealing with Uncertainty*

Financial planners always encourage their clients to evaluate their retirement goals and estimate how much money it will take them to live during the later stages of their lives. There are financial surveys with a series of questions that help indicate risk-taking attitudes. My financial advisor uses a basic rule of thumb to help gauge risk-taking decisions by asking a simple question: "can you sleep at night without worrying about your investments?" If a person is constantly looking at the stock market each day and frequently calling a financial advisor, she or he probably needs to change investment strategies.

> "More important than the quest for certainty is the quest for clarity."
>
> FRANCIS GAUTIER

Those who have learned to effectively work through unexpected setbacks reflect a unique perspective and understanding about decision making. Responding to the fact that life may (and often does) present people with unexpected situations they must deal with, companies have developed various products that offer certain compensations.

Insurance companies, for example, offer a wide range of plans involving individual products (like cameras), unique situations such as a surgeon's hands, or even corporate financial dealings. Individuals still must face the reality that different insurance plans only address a portion of life's risks. This fact highlights the need to develop wisdom, to perhaps have peace of mind in the midst of chaotic times.

Uncertainty generates situations that transcend common or familiar decision-making principles. These situations may require people to adapt to changing circumstances and develop new thinking models. Stephen S. Hall relates that "wisdom is not simply a matter of knowing the best answer to a problem or dilemma; it is a matter of knowing the best *approach* for finding the best answer." Hall considers the ability to deal with uncertainty a pillar of wisdom that enables people to break from relying upon past practices, tradition, and habits. In addition, certain temptations must be resisted: being quick, action oriented, emotionally driven, delay making a choice, selecting the most comfortable option, and focusing too much on either short or long term goals.

Sound judgments are based upon taking a fresh and flexible perspective. Embracing novel problem-solving strategies helps people make better decisions. Wisdom evolves into the art of coping and savoring each day.

Embracing novel problem-solving strategies help people to achieve better decisions.

"Whatever an education is, it should make you a unique individual, not a conformist; it should furnish you with an original spirit with which to tackle the big challenges; it should allow you to find values which will be your road map through life; it should make you spiritually rich, a person who loves whatever you are doing, wherever you are, whomever you are with; it should teach you what is important, how to live and how to die."

JOHN GATTO

Learning

14 *Boring Education*

John Gatto is an advocate for changing the nature of American education. He is a former New York City public school teacher dedicated to changing to how children are taught. Tragically, teachers leave the profession at an alarming rate, and there is a chronic problem with students dropping out of high school. I have concerns about American education promoting social conformity over individuality, creativity, and self-directed learning.

John Gatto discusses seven negative educational trends in his book *Dumbing us Down: The Hidden Curriculum of Compulsory Schooling.* The educational trends are undermining the teaching and learning process and reflect a lack of wisdom. I have provided commentary on Gatto's points:

❶ **Confusion** - subject matter is presented out of context, creating intellectual confusion. Lessons are disjointed and don't consider student interests and needs. The sequence of classes and subjects lack a rational purpose and often produce disjointed knowledge. The lack of adequate connections with concepts and ideas prevents students from developing a coherent view of knowledge.

② Class position - The stress on testing creates competition within schools and between students who know their place in the academic pyramid. Future employers probably will not be very concerned about test results, a fact ignored by educational leaders who constantly push for higher test scores.

③ Indifference - the school schedule of bells, frequent class interruptions, and changing classes reflects a culture built upon movement and brief encounters with learning. Daily activities are constrained by the absence of time for the deeper reading of materials and discussion of ideas. The message is clear: school work is not really important.

④ Emotional dependency - teachers use a punishment-and-reward system that fosters dependent attitudes. Teachers have enormous power and control over children that can diminish opportunities to express individuality and develop emotional independence.

⑤ Intellectual dependency - students are trained to listen to their teachers and are told what to do. Teachers judge the quality of work and direction of classroom schedule. There are limited opportunities to develo the capacity for self-directed work.

⑥ Provisional self-esteem - students are told their worth through tests, grades and report cards. The approach neglects personal evaluation and relies too heavily upon judgments of others.

⑦ No hiding place - children are placed under continuous surveillance, indicating to them that they should not be trusted. Controlling students transcends most privacy concerns.

Gatto offers some insights into why there has been growing frustration with American public schools. Reform efforts have consistently failed to improve the student's educational experiences. When I was a high school history teacher, the block schedule (ninety-minute class periods) made my job extremely difficult. The basic theory regarding block scheduling is that students will do better with more class time and fewer subjects.

In reality, it creates a host of instructional problems that undermine achievement. For instance, students struggling to learn math or English due to the rapid pace of the classes and a schedule that favors those who are already good at those subjects. Students struggle to maintain their concentration even with the best teachers.

The hour and half classes are not prepping students for college either because most college classes are not more than an hour in length. Research studies have failed to support the academic advantages of the block schedule. Sadly, this is just one example of how schools continue to implement flawed ideas and gimmicks. Student learning suffers and people grow more disillusioned with public education.

Alfie Kohn, in his book *Feel-Bad Education: And Other Contrarian Essays*

Student learning suffers and people grow more disillusioned with public education.

on Children and Schooling, classifies the current focus on academic rigor as the "Listerine theory of education" where the emphasis is selling the mouthwash based on the idea that if tasted bad enough, it must be good stuff. The stress on rigor appears to be partly driven by some fear that if students enjoy their learning experiences, it must not be "real" learning. The emphasis on "feel-bad" education reflects anxiety over the possibility of individuals finding excessive pleasure in learning. Kohn questions the emphasis on self-denial and the philosophy of suffering as the key to gaining knowledge.

School districts have eliminated recess and playground activities because more time is required for student-test preparations. Simon Blackburn observes that "When no time is left for the free play of the imagination, but learning is a matter of drudgery, and repetition, its success measured only economic ends of which the child has no comprehension, how should we expect any more than a sullen rejection, a rebellion against everything school and the adult world represent?"

In the future, American historians could describe the worship of standardized testing as a dark educational era. Classrooms could be known for their absence of joy, for being emotionally barren places where students suffered over meaningless work.

Educational leaders and political officials should consider the primary objectives of education. A major educational goal should involve preparing students to be self-directed learners who can actively participate in a democratic society. The excessive emphasis on testing undermines efforts to cultivate the critical thinking skills that are essential for the development of effective leaders. Reform efforts should focus on how to make learning more meaningful for students and better prepare them for their future. We need to develop schools with a new and vibrant vision of learning, one that sparks the students' imaginations and captures their hearts.

15 *Meaningful Learning*

Today's educational reformers fail to address the need for students to enjoy the learning process. The debate over classroom work reflects competing visions of what constitutes a good education. As a veteran educator, I find it tragic to watch bright, energetic young people become lethargic about their education. Perhaps the real problem lies with adults who lack a comprehensive view of learning.

> "Nothing is more terrible than activity without insight."
>
> THOMAS CARLYLE

Often, teachers and adults are guilty of classifying real learning as being a difficult and frustrating experience. The emphasis on testing in public schools reflects a narrow and rigid perspective on the teaching and learning process. A constant focus on preparing and taking tests is creating a generation of students who equate learning with test results. Students are learning a set of academic standards that create more followers and consumers, but fail at creating leaders and people with a spirit of adventure.

Those who advocate regular homework have a distorted outlook on the nature of learning. It is tragic that students are forced to work on long assignments while being robbed of time for play and family activities. A growing number of students complain that school is rarely fun and neglects to meet their needs. Yet, there are those who view homework as a positive way to help children who lack parental supervision in the late afternoons, saying homework helps them focus on productive activities and stay out of trouble. There is wisdom in having a balanced

Some of the most profound educational moments have occurred while my high school students were creating posters or playing games.

perspective on this issue. Children, of course, vary in their learning needs. The homework should be meaningful and intellectually challenging. We need to help young people to cultivate a vision of learning that sparks their imagination and captures their hearts. Some of the most profound educational moments have occurred while my high school students were creating posters or playing games. Learning should be a joy, not a burden.

John Dewey's vision of education is future oriented, focused on preparing students for an uncertain future. Dewey was an educational pioneer in learning by doing. He thought students should work with real problems. He rejected what he considered to be the spectator approach to learning where individuals acquire knowledge but fail to apply the information in the world. The classroom is a community for preparing students for participating in democratic institutions. A relevant curriculum meets student needs by being aligned with their developmental state.

In *Democracy and Education*, Dewey discusses how teachers who try to share and transfer knowledge without adequate student engagement in the teaching and learning process are creating situations that produce a form of "static, cold storage knowledge." He wanted schools to be alive with constant opportunities for personal development, reflective thinking, and acquisition of a vision for social involvement in a democratic society. A primary goal of education, Dewey theorized, is to cultivate critical thinking habits and the social construction of knowledge.

16 Teachers

Teachers are often targeted for educational reform efforts that are designed to improve the quality of education. One underlying assumption of all reform efforts is the idea of deficiency and developing prescribed formulas that will resolve educational problems. Teachers will always judge the potential changes according to whether the ideas can be translated into their daily instructional routines. Educators become frustrated when school officials expect them to make curriculum changes without engaging in any serious dialogue regarding their plans.

Andy Hargreaves observes that "change devices usually rely on principles of compulsion, constraint or contrivance to get teachers to change." Teachers need relevant professional growth activities that foster best teaching practices and not activities based on the latest

> "One looks back with appreciation to the brilliant teachers, but with gratitude to those who touched our human feelings. The curriculum is so much necessary raw material, but warmth is the vital element for the growing plant and for the soul of the child."
>
> CARL JUNG

> Schools must make mentoring educators a higher priority.

fad. Change for the sake of change can create more problems and fail to improve the quality of teaching.

As an educator, it disturbs me to witness the decline of public schools and their inability to offer quality learning experiences. Teachers suffer from an absence of parental support and students who lack a work ethic and respect for others. Educational reformers advocate better teacher-education programs, and these programs can play a vital role in reforming education. Schools must make mentoring educators a higher priority. Michael Fullan and other writers recognize the important role teachers play and realize that changes must be made to develop a learning culture that attracts and rewards the best teachers for their achievements.

Unfortunately, our educational systems are designed to promote conformity, not creativity. Seth Godin states that "The problem is that most schools don't like great teachers. They're organized to stamp them out, bureaucratize them, and make them average." Social conformity in higher education can happen to teachers who display exceptional talents. As a university teacher, I recall being disciplined by an administrator who took a negative perspective on my publishing achievements. The administrator punished me by reducing my teaching load.

There is a growing risk of qualified people leaving the teaching profession due to being in school environments that reward mediocrity and punish excellence. An excessive focus on conformity restricts the development of wisdom because people are more hesitant to share ideas and best practices. There is less incentive for teachers to excel when the culture fails to support superior work.

17 *Educational Goals*

American educators face a diversity of expectations from a various stakeholders. The federal government, state legislatures, and local school districts are the major stakeholders with the power to establish priorities such as curriculum objectives and standards. Also, textbook publishers exert influence through their materials that play a role in guiding instruction in classrooms The presence of competing visions on the purposes of education have made teaching a complicated endeavor. Educators can integrate relevancy into their instruction by considering the ultimate purposes of learning even as they strive to meet mandated educational directives.

> "Accept the challenges, so you may feel the exhilaration of victory."
>
> GENERAL GEORGE PATTON

The university classes I teach always include activities and discussions arising from student needs. This requires taking the time to learn my students' goals and daily challenges. Course objectives are always the primary guiding light for lesson plans. Yet, within the instructional objectives are opportunities to share ideas and activities that help students develop enduring skills and knowledge that transcend their educational setting. With the following list, I offer descriptions of the characteristics I hope the work I assign will help my students develop:

1. **Quest for knowledge** - comfortable with ambiguity, strong intellectual curiosity, enjoys reading across the academic disciplines.

2. **Discipline** - good work ethic, dedicated, determined, able to complete difficult tasks in a timely manner.

3. **Goal oriented** - creates short- and long-term learning goals, daily activities affirm values and priorities, develops professional growth plans that affirm a passion for learning.

4. **Communication skills** - written and verbal messages are clear and meaningful, effectively connects with a diversity of people, intellectual who engages in social issues.

5. **Independence** - autonomous, self-motivated, self-directed, uses solitude to cultivate expertise and reflect on deeper life issues.

6. **Humility** - meekness (power under control), teachable, appreciates personal abilities and the talents of others, rejoices with people who excel and has empathy for those who experience setbacks.

7. **Wisdom** - sound judgments, emotional resilience, able to cope with adversity, aware of the limitations of knowledge.

8. **Research skills** - able to create original research projects, develop reflective literature reviews, and effectively share results with others.

9. **Critical/Creative thinking skills** - regulates thinking, fosters creativity and problem solving skills, cultural creator who shares ideas and knowledge with others.

10. **Leadership skills** - good character, competent, a caring communicator, generates hope, inspires excellence in others, visionary.

The wise consider life a learning adventure filled with challenging experiences and opportunities to help others.

Educators can integrate relevancy into their instruction by considering the ultimate purposes of learning while striving to meet the educational directives from various stakeholders. Each day supplies new situations requiring wisdom and unique problem-solving skills. Teachers can bring a slice of reality into their daily instruction through the use of creative activities.

For instance, students could use Google to identify interesting wisdom quotes and generate creative wisdom stories based on one or two quotes. The lesson could help the class understand some of the wonderful benefits of acquiring wisdom. Students who are anxious at times will gain insights into how the wise acquire confidence and enjoy each day. They may discover that the wise consider life a learning adventure filled with challenging experiences and opportunities to help others.

18   *Higher Education: Genuine Teaching and Learning*

It is interesting to observe teachers who claim to be student-centered in their educational philosophy but reflect controlling behaviors in their classes. Teachers can dominate online dialogs by posting an excessive number of messages highlighting the instructor's expertise but undermining communication and student learning. Instructors can become threatened by the open-ended quality of the online setting, which causes some individuals to strive for security through greater control.

Sadly, students are receiving an academically weaker education. There is frustration with instructors who fail to share their expertise, who foster superficial discussions. Students wonder about the quality of their ideas because the teacher fails to create a genuine dialog that affirms the worth of the students' questions and concerns.

Students vary in their cognitive maturity, and educators must develop a set of flexible techniques and lesson plans that will help them to meet a diversity of student needs. Teachers should foster a rich intellectual environment by

> "Since there is no single set of abilities running throughout human nature, there is no single curriculum which all should undergo. Rather, the schools should teach everything that anyone is interested in learning."
>
> JOHN DEWEY

66   WISDOM: *Making Good Choices with Imperfect Knowledge*

Teachers can promote lively discussions by creating discussion questions that encourage critical thinking and stimulate student contributions.

creating a more personal, less-formal class structure. An informal class can encourage independent learning projects built around student interests while promoting creativity, reflective thinking, and self-directed learning. It is important that teachers enable students to have the freedom to ask questions and take intellectual risks in their assignments and class discussions. Teachers can promote lively discussions by creating discussion questions that encourage critical thinking and stimulate student contributions.

Online students want to experience the human side of learning. The online environment can be lonely at times, and students want to get to know their teachers and classmates. Students can enjoy teacher stories that make the class more personal and perhaps clarify certain aspects of their academic work. Stories can build bridges between theory and practice and make principles more memorable.

Fred White notes that "when we tell stories of our lives, we are in a sense, shaping them into meaningful units; we are framing them, inviting others to pay closer attention to them."

Instructors can promote participation by affirming their students' abilities and knowledge. The teacher can make positive comments about an individual's expertise, publicly in a newsgroup or other discussion forum or privately in email messages. The key is to be sincere and share positive comments with every student in the class. Learners appreciate being recognized for their accomplishments, and online classes offer numerous opportunities for instructors to affirm quality work.

19 *Online University Dialogs*

The online setting or distance learning environment holds potential for vibrant interaction and rich dialog. Unfortunately, online educational experiences can become quite wooden and lifeless at times, similar to a boring traditional classroom. Distance educators and their students can become disillusioned with the teaching and learning process when it lacks a dynamic, interactive character. A rigid online learning environment will often fail to acknowledge the need for individualized and context-sensitive learning. The educational model should offer flexibility for instructors and students to interact freely.

> "The courage to imagine the otherwise is our greatest resource, adding color and suspense to all our life."
>
> DANIEL BOORSTIN

Today's students want online classes that are enjoyable places where learning expectations are built upon relevant intellectual activities and discussions. Students are given extremely detailed instructions on assignments that leave little room for creative approaches to completing the work.

The level of cognitive maturity will vary among students which will require having teachers to make creative adaptations to their teaching plans and activities. Curriculum changes should not reduce the academic quality of the course work. Online degree program administrators must

Online degree program administrators must avoid the temptation to dumb down their curriculum standards to increase their student enrollment numbers.

avoid the temptation to dumb down their curriculum standards to increase their student enrollment numbers.

The lowering of educational standards appears to help more students experience a measure of academic success. It really represents a patronizing view of people that questions their ability to effectively take on new intellectual challenges and it reflects an ambiguous view of equity. Frank Furedi says "by treating people as weak and vulnerable individuals who are likely to stumble when confronted by intellectual challenge, such cultural attitudes serve to create a culture of low expectations." Distance education administrators, admission personnel and teachers need to work together to maintain high intellectual expectations for their students and uphold the academic integrity of their institutions.

Instructors can promote greater online participation by affirming their students' abilities and knowledge. The teacher can make positive comments about an individuals' expertise in the discussion forum. The key is to be sincere and share positive comments with every student in the class. Adult learners appreciate being recognized for their accomplishments and online classes offer numerous opportunities for instructors to affirm quality work.

The online environment can be lonely at times due to the absence of sharing in a face to face setting. Students want to get to know their teachers and classmates. A best teaching practice involves having instructors and their students share biographical posts during the first few days of class. An informative biography will highlight data that offers insights into the individual's life.

This is simple procedure that can humanize the online class by helping students learn more about their teacher and colleagues. Students can use the biographical posts as a reference point to communicate during the course. Teachers can share stories related to subject matter to make the class more personal and assist students with their academic work.

The wise instructor will use short stories to generate lively discussions. Also, stories can be used to share advice about professional growth and future careers. Yet, personal narratives should never replace the actual instruction of the subject matter. Teachers should develop a class structure that stimulates social interaction, affirms academic standards and makes learning an enjoyable experience. I think online students want classes that stress the human side of learning. The online environment can be lonely at times and students want to get to know their teachers and classmates. Students really enjoy stories from the teacher's life because they make the class more personal.

20 Doctoral Studies

People can pursue a doctoral degree for a variety of personal and professional reasons. The excessive focus on tenure has created a very limited traditional higher education job market for those who fail to acquire tenure. The current amount of time to earn a doctoral degree in English and the humanities is ten years. The research literature continually highlights that over 50% who pursue a doctoral do not complete their degree and are classified as All But Dissertation (ABD).

> "The quality of a university is measured more by the kind of student it turns out than the kind it takes in."
>
> ROBERT J. KIBBEE

Sadly, the traditional higher educational system is equipped for producing ABD's and keeping graduate students available as cheap labor for teaching undergraduate classes. Also, only about half of those who earn a traditional doctoral degree will secure a tenured college position. Louis Menard notes that "there is a huge social inefficiency in taking people of high intelligence and devoting resources to training them in programs that half will never complete and for jobs that most will not get."

The system discourages risk taking and has created politically rigid academic departments. The majority of today's college professors are Democrats. In my opinion, this should raise some concerns about the intellectual integrity of their hiring processes. Teachers are concerned about their status as administrators hire fewer tenured instructors and

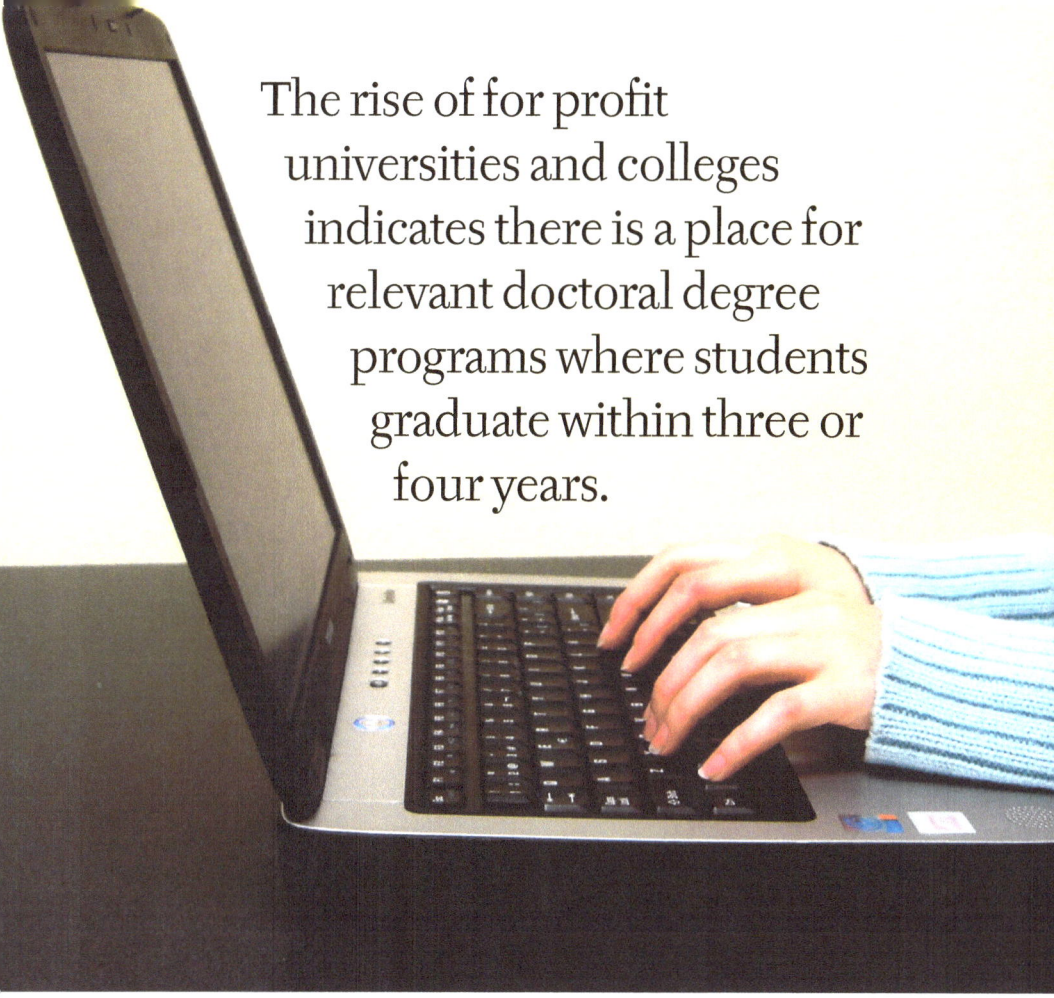

> The rise of for profit universities and colleges indicates there is a place for relevant doctoral degree programs where students graduate within three or four years.

rely more upon adjuncts. Academic disciplines wrestle with being relevant while immersed in arguments over trivial procedural matters. Teachers wonder about being part of organizations that struggle to be innovative while appearing almost indifferent to making significant changes.

The rise of for-profit universities and colleges indicates there is a place for relevant doctoral degree programs where students graduate within three or four years. Those who dream of having a doctoral degree should be given the opportunity to pursue this noble endeavor. Perhaps there is a need for more Ph.D.'s who can use their expertise and knowledge to work on designing creative solutions to social problems. Our society can benefit from interacting with individuals who understand how to identify and retrieve relevant information which is important for making wise decisions.

21 *Writing*

Writing can be a dynamic way of communicating and sharing wisdom. Each person must identify his or her motivation for writing. Perhaps, individuals have received encouragement to write from college professors, friends and colleagues. Yet, there could be some hesitation because of concerns about time constraints in creating an article, poems, or books due to fears of rejection. It is important to face these concerns and realize that developing confidence will require taking some risks and developing realistic writing plans.

Sharing stories can be a powerful way to relate principles and sustain reader interest. Stories play an essential role in developing contextual information, enlarging personal frames of reference, offering more accurate information, and helping readers identify with the subject. A story affirms the human perspective and encourages awareness about social issues and the potential for growth

> "If my doctor told me I had only six minutes to live, I wouldn't brood. I'd type a little faster."
>
> ISAAC ASIMOV

During my academic journey, a variety of people have encouraged me to publish. Yet, it was not until after completing my second doctoral degree that writing for publication became a reality.

My first attempt at publishing was not successful but was a valuable learning experience. The topic did not fit the journal's focus. This experience prompted me to devote more time to exploring journals to identify places to share my ideas. It is important to invest time into studying various publications before making a final decision on a topic and place of submission. Deborah S. Ray recommends the writer asks himself or herself some specific questions regarding the journal being approached:

1. What is its purpose?

2. What regular departments or features does it include?

3. What seasonal material does it include?

4. What range of freelance-written topics does it cover?

5. What topics and articles have been recently published?

6. What elements and features do the articles include?

7. What writing techniques, structure, and organization do authors employ?

8. How long are the articles?

9. How deep is the information?

10. How do articles and accompanying graphics appear?

11. How formal or informal are the design, writing, and graphics?

Ray's list of questions will help individuals to identify the potential journals or magazines that offer the best publication opportunities. The next step is to establish a series of short- and long-term writing goals. Writing can be a personal endeavor of wanting to explore subjects at a deeper level. Creating goals provides direction and encourages integrating writing into daily routines. Learning to write on a regular basis requires being creative, disciplined, and having a strong interest or passion for the subject.

It is vital to seize good ideas and immediately start writing. Creating an idea journal is a way to capture thoughts that arise from brainstorming or appear unexpectedly. This may increase productivity by developing knowledge insights into journal articles, lecture notes, mind maps and letters to the editor.

Ralph Waldo Emerson would often read five hours a day and the habit helped him produce thought-provoking literature. Writers need to devote more effort and time in critical reading of the literature before sharing with the public. Stephen King's book *On Writing: A Memoir of the Craft* is a wonderful resource that is informative, inspiring, and full of excellent advice.

Sharing stories can be a powerful way to relate principles and sustain reader interest. Stories play an essential role in developing contextual information, enlarging personal frames of reference, offering more

> Learning to write on a regular basis requires being creative, disciplined and having a strong interest or passion for the subject.

accurate information, and helping readers identify with the subject. A story affirms the human perspective and encourages awareness about social issues and the potential for growth.

Socrates is often cited as an example of a wise person because he recognized the limits of personal knowledge. He would ask people questions as a way for them to learn how to better monitor their thinking by identifying flaws such as bias. Socrates used intense question sessions to offer lessons for those willing to learn.

Often, he taught there is wisdom and humility in being aware of one's knowledge limitations. Then, individuals will see the need to study a subject more deeply and appreciate those who have expertise. The Socratic Method of asking questions remains a popular teaching technique.

Editors are always looking for creative articles that will meet the needs of their readers. Writers should strive to develop positive relationships with editors by submitting quality work, meeting promised deadlines, and responding promptly to e-mail or telephone messages. Individuals should avoid dwelling on fears about rejection and focus on preparing their best work. Writing for publication represents wonderful opportunities to challenge conventional thinking, advocate changes, share best practices, and encourage others.

22 *Creative Writing*

Today's technologies has given new meaning to the importance of writing. People will text messages, post remarks on personal websites, share on social networking sites (e.g. Facebook) and email their colleagues, business associates and friends. The communication requires various forms of formal and informal writing depending upon the social context.

Writing skills can be improved through self evaluation, practice and feedback. Individuals can share their written work with others and relate their need to have specific guidance (e.g. passive sentences) which encourages more relevant advice. Writing insights on grammar and style issues are available through books (e.g. Royal's, 2004 *The Little Red Writing Book;* Strunk & White's *Elements of Style)* and grammar software programs. A writer that uses a thesaurus will give new life to narratives.

Arthur Plotnik shares six advantages of using the thesaurus:

> "Be a Columbus to whole new continents and worlds within you, opening new channels, not of trade, but of thought."
>
> HENRY DAVID THOREAU

1. Discover more fitting or more forceful words;
2. Find those good words you can't quite recall;
3. Avoid repetition of words;

4 Escape clichés and worn modifiers;

5 Help describe the so-called indescribable;

6 Refine your intended meanings (via related concepts)

Take the time to investigate words, use dictionaries to look up meanings and reflect on why authors select certain terms. The goal is never to impress the reader with large or exotic words. Rather, language should be clear, interesting and informative. Stephen Wilbers states *"The secret to connecting with your reader is to be yourself. It may take confidence, even courage, to reveal who you are, but your reader wants to know. Don't hide behind your words."*

Being yourself will foster genuine communication of thoughts. People long for personal and honest conversations. Using artificial language creates credibility issues because it might not be clear what the author truly believes. Those who struggle with grammar issues can become so absorbed with avoiding mistakes which can diminish their message. This can cause the message to become distorted or creates distance from the reader and undermines the writer's credibility.

How can writing become more dynamic and personal? The key is to integrate personality traits into writing by being genuine, lively, and somewhat playful at times... and even unpredictable. People long to encounter personal narratives where the writer shares the challenges in struggling to understand complex ideas and problems. I believe readers are able to connect with those who have similar struggles.

Writers can infuse personality into the text by using action verbs and visual terms that generate colorful images. For instance, when discussing a major concept, instead of implementing the traditional rational approach, share a metaphor and appeal to the reader's imagination. Writing for personal or professional reasons can be an adventure in creativity.

Creative writing involves having a level of confidence in one self and being able to generate new ideas, communicating the thoughts into a engaging narrative. Yet, why are some people able to write more freely than others who struggle to produce work? Perhaps, it has to do with their creative confidence mindset. Researchers tested 1,300 people across diverse industries and indentified six major traits that fostered creativity. I have highlighted the key points of Amantha Imber's studies:

1. **Open to experience** - people who enjoy variety in their daily lives and pursue new experiences, have a strong curiosity and active imagination which enables them to be creative at work.

2. **Creative self-efficacy** - an individual's confidence in their ability to generate creative ideas, seek problem-oriented tasks and have a strong belief in being able to produce the best ideas. This self-belief plays a vital role in motivation for creative thinking.

3. **Resilience** - refers to being able to respond positively to adversity or disappointments with a positive attitude and determination to continue working on their plans. Those who possess resilience can see value in failure as well as rejection, and are significantly more creative at their work.

4. **Confidence in intuition** - this is often called "gut thinking" or feeling that relies upon making automatic judgments. This approach is in contrast to the much slower and deliberate *analytical* thinking. Being confident in the intuitive decisions has a positive impact on fostering creativity.

5. **Tolerance of ambiguity** - enjoys the challenge of engaging in open-ended problem solving situations and tasks. Individuals embrace ambiguity because it offers opportunities for autonomy and the flexibility to work through dynamic problems.

6. **Cross application of experiences** - drawing upon experiences not related to work as a resource for applying knowledge in new and creative ways.

Writers can use the six creative traits as a guide for improving their ability to generate novel and original thinking for their writing projects. For instance, the weekly routines might need to be changed by selecting new places to have a meal or try reading a different literature genre. Also, the creative author needs to be open to different experiences, so as to remain mentally and emotionally fresh.

This book challenged me to learn to handle the discomfort of writing in a new and unfamiliar format. A great deal of my publications have been in journals. Creating this book gave me new opportunities to communicate in a different style. It took time to choose the best approach to showcase the vast subject of wisdom.

Robert Sternberg relates that "a creative idea tends to come in bits and pieces and develops over time. But the period when the idea is developing is often uncomfortable." What did help me during the transition from journal articles to this book was reading and studying the nature of creativity. The literature continually reminded me that the creative process demands persistence, especially when apparently hitting dead ends in the search for solutions. It requires having a hopeful mindset that patiently and enthusiastically waits for the best ideas and solutions.

Seeing

23 *Science Fiction Insights*

What is science fiction? A helpful definition of this popular term is from Sam Moskowitz: "A branch of fantasy identifiable by the fact that it eases the 'willing suspension of disbelief' on the part of its readers by utilizing an atmosphere of scientific credibility for its imaginative speculations in physical science, space, time, social science, and philosophy."

The definition acknowledges how vast an array of subjects science fiction touches. Films and literature often stress how individuals and groups strive for a better life but are frequently thwarted. As new technologies emerge, we often find that they're a mixed blessing. For instance, Phillip Dick's dystopian

> "Learning and innovation go hand in hand. The arrogance of success is to think that what you did yesterday will be sufficient for tomorrow."
>
> WILLIAM POLLARD

> Book burning is a direct attack on the idea of individuality and the determination to maintain social conformity.

society describes those who have survived a nuclear war and find comfort in electronic sheep. Science fiction literature represents a range of ideas involving people and intelligent machines struggling through life and death experiences. In *Blade Runner*, readers are prompted to have empathy for the machines who display human traits such as emotions.

20th-century science fiction writers have been skeptical about utopian or ideal societies. Aldous Huxley's *Brave New World* and George Orwell's *1984* reflect fears about totalitarian states which control people's thinking and represent an anti-utopian perspective known as dystopia. Jeff Prucher describes dystopia as "an imagined society or state of affairs in which conditions are extremely bad, especially in which these conditions result from the continuation of some current trend to an extreme...."

Dystopian scenarios reflect how current trends (e.g. mass media) taken to extremes can create horrible outcomes. A popular dystopian theme involves the use of harsh measures to control people and their daily lives. In Bradbury's *Fahrenheit 451*, the elimination of reading had a negative impact on language by making it more difficult to learn new words. Book burning is a direct attack on the idea of individuality and the determination to maintain social conformity. The novel reflects the fears of having weapons that can destroy civilizations and the existence of oppressive societies which repeat the terrible mistakes of previous generations.

Bradbury's (1953) *Fahrenheit 451* shares a vision of a dystopian society that experiences nuclear war as an opportunity for social renewal. The book closes with the possibility of another nuclear war.

The novel places a major focus on Guy Montag who lives in a futuristic American city, and chronicles his dramatic change from a hard-working fireman who burns books into a member of the underground library movement that preserves books. The novel describes Montag's journey of personal development that starts with his book-burning work. As time progresses, he begins to doubt the wisdom of destroying books.

Captain Beatty, a fellow fireman, has conversations with Montag designed to provide a history of fire-fighting and offer justification for firemen's activities. Beatty has read a diversity of books and is able to identify the sources of Montag's knowledge, arguing against saving books because they contain contradictory information and create greater uncertainty about life. Beatty states, "Stick with the firemen, Montag. All else is dreary chaos!"

Science fiction offers futuristic visions about the role of leaders and technology planning. Howard E. McCurdy notes that "works of science fiction provide a fresh and often useful perspective on the ethics of vision-making and transformational leadership. They place among the requirements of ethical leadership a sensitivity to the consequences of one's vision-making." The hope of producing a better future through technologies could have unintended negative consequences. There are warnings about striving to control others and their surroundings excessively.

Utopian visions about progress can be flawed and leaders can lose sight of using technologies for the common good. The philosophical dimension of science fiction raises significant moral questions about the future, as leaders are exhorted to explore their plans and ask more "what if" questions. Major science fiction themes involve the absence of wisdom, promoting anti-intellectualism, diminished expectations and superficial relationships. These topics have enduring value as people embrace new technologies and create social networks.

Have science fiction films had a positive or negative effect on fostering wisdom? In the past, people would read literature and the writers would use metaphors and word pictures to spark the reader's imagination. Reading a novel requires a personal investment of time and emotional energy. Watching a film does have a passive dimension, but there are opportunities to be reflective while exploring social issues and relationships while asking philosophical questions. Films and reading each play a valid role in entertainment and learning. Each has the potential for cultivating an active imagination that fosters creativity and problem-solving, both of which are wisdom traits.

Watching a film does have a passive dimension but there are opportunities to be reflective...

24 *Blogs*

A popular definition among bloggers is Tim Jarret's: "blogs are personally published documents on the web, with attribution and date, collected in a single place, generally published with a static structure to facilitate incoming links from other sources, and updated with some regularity and frequency… " The author can control the content through the process of posting comments, editing, revising and deleting materials.

The power to control content and the ability to reach a national and international audience make blogging an appealing and dynamic endeavor. Bloggers are known for their playful personas dedicated to sharing their opinion with others. Cognitive psychologists have recognized an important paradox in creative accomplishments involving playfulness and discipline.

Creative individuals work very hard and continue their work with a level of persistence rarely matched by others. They often possess playful attitudes which help them evaluate ideas with an abandonment and imagination. Their ability to find joy in their work enables them to take necessary breaks from the serious business of pondering complex ideas. Creative people have learned how to foster a receptive mental outlook that helps them produce novel concepts or ideas in this digital world.

> "We find comfort among those who agree with us—growth among those who don't."
>
> FRANK A. CLARK

People can use other bloggers to test their ideas on. Group interaction can be a foundation for creativity in education and business organizations. The blogosphere can foster creativity by integrating learning, professional practice and research on social and educational issues. Information is presented within the community which stimulates dialog by asking thought-provoking questions.

The merging of content and discussion offers numerous opportunities to examine and explore new ideas. Also, the discussions can be quite dynamic over extended periods of time. Individuals can take time to reflect and devote additional time investigating a topic before posting their comments. Blogger dialogs stimulate intellectual risk-taking as well.

An important characteristic among bloggers is their spirit of adventure and willingness to share information. The blogosphere contains tens of thousands of people who enjoy informal learning outside of higher education. Bloggers develop information networks that offer both generalized and specialized information that supports lifelong learning and acquiring wisdom insights.

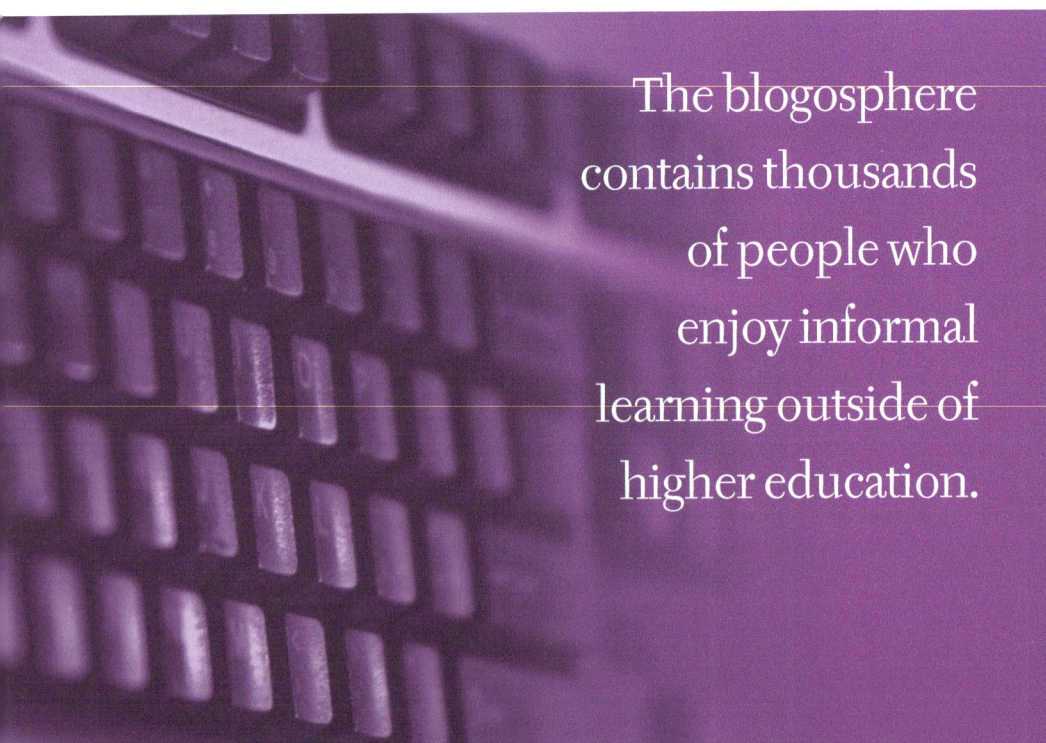

The blogosphere contains thousands of people who enjoy informal learning outside of higher education.

25 Blog Popularity

The formal print media through journals, newspapers and magazines continues to supply an important avenue for exchanging ideas within the academic world. Blogs reflect a powerful new communication tool that provides an intellectual leveling effect that invites participation from people who represent more diverse backgrounds.

Too, today's blogs often function as a practical technological format for creating professional bridges between people across and within academic disciplines. Blogs appeal to people because they offer an opportunity to share life experiences, vent frustrations and reflect on a variety of social issues. Contemporary life can be quite impersonal, and people long to have opportunities to express themselves to others in an environment that they construct.

Blogging offers educators an excellent platform to forge their

> "The task before us is to extend into the digital world the virtues of authenticity, expertise, and scholarly apparatus that have evolved over the 500 years of print, virtues often absent in the manuscript age that preceded print."
>
> MICHAEL GORMAN

own professional identity by sharing with other colleagues and debating ideas. Henry Farrell argues that "Academic blogs, like their 18th-century equivalent, are rife with feuds, displays of spleen, crotchets, fads, and nonsenses. As in the blogosphere more generally, there is a lot of dross. However, academic blogs also provide a carnival of ideas, a lively and exciting interchange of argument and debate that makes many scholarly conversations seem drab and desiccated in comparison."

Educators who are interested in using blogs can enhance their professional growth by utilizing material related to their specific academic field, sharing instructional ideas with those who have similar interests. Blogs can be used to exchange course announcements, readings and relevant information links.

As blogs become more sophisticated and organized on the Internet, they will play a larger role in knowledge management for both teachers and students. Teachers should explore opportunities to use blogs in their classes, such as having students write reflective journals, create e-portfolios, examine definitions of terms, and conduct learning team assignments.

Blogs have a diversity of educational benefits, such as helping students understand and construct new knowledge, use computers to design products, and become acquainted with new technologies that can increase their productivity. Students can cultivate skills and knowledge that foster autonomy and confidence, both of which are essential for school and work.

Blogging represent a dynamic and growing activity among professionals and students who appreciate blogs for their mix of informal commentary, links to resources and their personal touch. Every blog carries a unique character that makes its distinct contribution to the Internet. Stephen Downes relates that "… a blog is also characterized by its reflection of a personal style, and this style may be reflected in either the writing or the selection of links passed along to readers. Blogs are the purest form, the core of what has come to be called personal publishing."

Technology is providing a virtual community to which organizes people to help others and provides information resources to gather data to share with public officials. During the 2008 election, blogs were used effectively to raise money for presidential candidates. In fact, over 3 million people contributed to Barack Obama campaign through the Internet.

Social networks can be a source for social change due to their ability to organize and focus on specific issues, but the interaction can sometimes be less meaningful and foster illusionary types of social involvement. Asaf Bar-tura observes "Facebook, like other public spheres, offers relatively passive ways of civic involvement which nevertheless give us a false sense of activity and accomplishment." Citizenship, I think, is sustained through dedication and active participation in the democratic process.

Blogs are changing how people create and share knowledge, but new technologies have been a mixed blessing. There are more online educational opportunities for training and obtaining degrees and developing new social relationships, yet the darker side of the new social media has raised concerns about sharing reliable information about individuals and products and identify theft. Parents worry about cyber-bullying and protecting their children. Internet communities are evolving rapidly and represent a new social frontier. Blogs do have the potential to foster sharing of ideas, encourage political participation, affirm democratic ideals, and promote the cultivation of wisdom.

As blogs become more sophisticated and organized on the Internet, they will play a larger role in knowledge management for both teachers and students.

26 *Children's Television Shows*

Media influence on children has often raised concerns about whether it has a negative influence on them. Critics fear that youth who watch television will be more isolated from others. Richard J. Harris relates that "…research has shown no relationship between the amount of television watched and time spent in interpersonal activity." The literature on media and children reveals a growing body of sophisticated insights which reveal the complexity of the issues.

Researchers have found that children recall stories from radio and television differently. Children related television stories with a greater degree of vagueness and also neglected detailed information from their radio narratives. It is speculated that television stories reflect similarities to a face-to-face conversation where individuals make a set of knowledge assumptions. Radio and printed material reflect the need to create a more detailed description of events to alleviate the absence of visual images.

The potential exists for television to encourage the cultivation of learning and positive educational outcomes. Mr. Rogers and Sesame Street are educational programs which promote positive learning experiences. Seasame Street programs have been shown to produce an assortment of positive learning outcomes for children, most notably in short-term effects. Students displayed improvement in their vocabulary,

> "The real voyage of discovery consists not in seeking new lands, but in seeing with new eyes."
>
> MARCEL PROUST

pre-reading skills and the cultivation of non-racist attitudes. Longitudinal studies reveal that the show has a particularly positive impact on student work in English, Math, and Science. Minority children experienced an increase in personal confidence and cultural pride.

Parents who discussed aspects of the show with their children as teachable opportunities did enhance the program's positive educational effects. It is also notable that studies have found children television programs can sometimes have negative educational results. The investigators examined a series of 10 television shows, including the popular Barney and Friends. The TV characters failed to properly use terms (e.g. think or know), and this created confusion in the children's minds about the meaning of words, hindering their vocabulary development. Television writers play a key role in creating instructionally sound episodes.

> Critics feared that youth who watch television will be more isolated from others.

The controversy over media violence among researchers involves interpretation of statistical information and the issue of multiple causes for any particular human behavior. Jennings Bryant acknowledges that the controversy continues, but that "…the research results reveal a dominant and consistent pattern in favor of the notion that exposure to violent media images does increase the risk of aggressive behavior."

Parents need to seize teachable moments with their children to help them learn discernment about the images and messages presented in television shows. Relevant role models at home and in the media can demonstrate how to handle conflicts and differences of opinions with others constructively. It is imperative that the nation's children learn to become discerning individuals who understand the nature of the media and how it can influence human behavior. Educators and parents must help children cultivate reflective skills and provide opportunities for them to experience the joys of creativity.

27 Media Stars

Today the public is quite familiar with the concept of celebrity, which often attributes fame to an individual for what they do outside of their work. The celebrity persona is really a mass media creation that is built through gossip, various reports in a host of magazines, and television shows such as Entertainment Tonight and the stars' public relations staff.

The celebrity status offers individuals ready access to elite parties, special seating at sporting events and movie premieres which increase their public visibility. The constant media attention reflects how much people want to know about the leisure activities and private life of their stars. The celebrity mode allows stars to have fame that transcends failures in their films. Contemporary fame is considerably different from earlier historical eras.

During the Renaissance, people diligently pursued public affirmation of their work. Fame was closely tied to genuine achievement, and people would strive for fame because it was considered a noble pursuit. The work of artists was financially supported by patrons who were often wealthy merchants, rich families, guilds and religious leaders. The patrons would hold a contest for major art projects and each of the competing artists would bring samples of their work. Then, patrons would select the individual who would be paid to complete their project.

> "Fame is a vapor, popularity an accident, and riches take wings. Only one thing endures and that is character."
>
> HORACE GREELEY

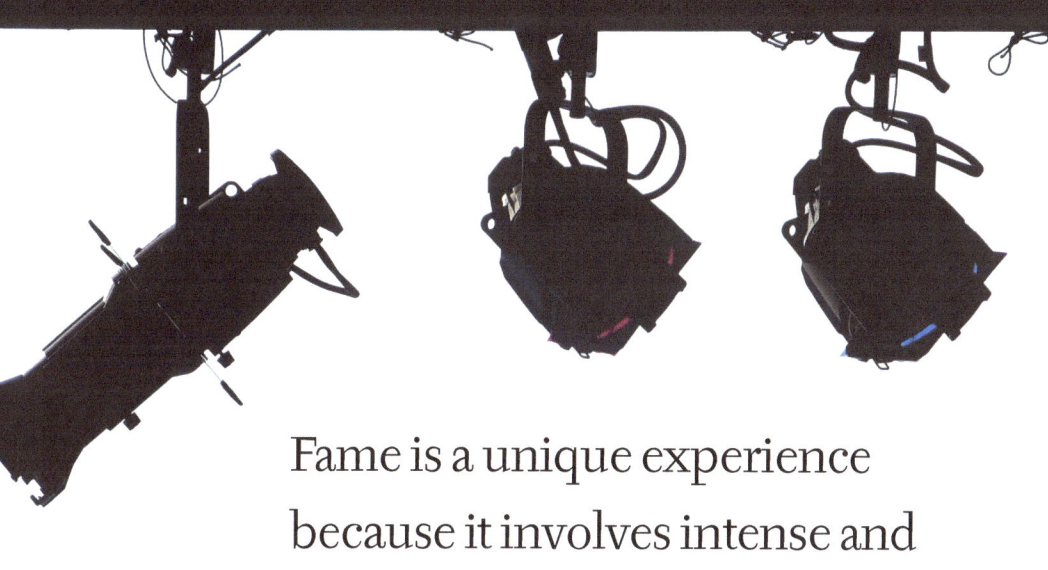

Fame is a unique experience because it involves intense and exciting media attention.

Actors can experience enormous popularity, including the excitement of being on talk shows and having their pictures in magazines. Americans want their stars to be fairly accessible; this can be a blessing that helps launch a film career or it can burden for actors who want more privacy. The desire for momentary fame is appealing when television producers give enticing financial rewards to those who are willing to do outrageous stunts.

Today, a growing number of reality television shows are gathering eager participants by offering them instant fame to perform before TV cameras. Yet, people can become disillusioned with their TV exposure because it does not always meet their expectations.

Fame is a unique experience because it involves intense and exciting media attention. After the media attention, individuals must often return to daily lives that are far more routine and less glamorous. Ultimately, there is wisdom in striving for genuine achievement and finding the inner satisfaction that comes from a life dedicated to personal excellence. Fame is fleeting, but character endures the test of time.

Being

28 *Social Conformity*

Cultural influences do impact how people view their world and their life. It is important for individuals to cultivate their reflective thinking skills to filter information. Matthew Lipman states "...critical thinking is skillful, responsible thinking that facilitates good judgment because it (1) relies upon criteria, (2) is self-correcting, and (3) is sensitive to context."

> "Character is always lost when a high ideal is sacrificed on the altar of conformity and popularity."
>
> ANONYMOUS

Critical thinking requires mental effort and the personal discipline to work with complex problems. Individuals with a critical spirit are often inquisitive about the mysteries of life and strive to find the most reliable information—for instance, reflecting on Os Guiness and how television shows often contain four major kinds of bias that influence their messages:

The Bias of TV

❶ It has bias against understanding because it stresses images and emotions but it often lacks context and meaning that creates an illusion of knowledge.

❷ Television conversations have a bias against responsibility by having a rapid approach that packages news into segments of intense images of dramatic events.

❸ Programs have a bias against historical events because news reports are focused on today as being far more important than the past.

❹ Television shows have a bias against rationality because attention is on performance by high profile individuals who prefer drama over reflective thought.

Americans have settled for a superficial creativity built upon passively observing others display their imagination through the entertainment industry. Business executives have managed to work creativity into neat film or television show formulas that are financially profitable, but fail to intellectually challenge people to be truly reflective and autonomous thinkers. Curtis White relates "The culture informed by the strategies of the Middle Mind promises intelligence, seriousness, care, but what it provides in reality is something other. What the Middle Mind does is flatten distinctions. It turns culture into mush."

Individual creativity is the result of making it a practice to take a fresh perspective on daily life. Each day holds a promise of a new beginning and unique encounters with ideas from others. Boredom is seldom a problem for those who want to improve their thinking and decision-making.

There is wisdom in regularly engaging in solitude. These can be valuable moments to mediate, reflect and recharge the emotional batteries. Solitude enables people to step back from their busy schedules to evaluate their priorities and goals. Perhaps it could be a time to creatively seek ways to develop deeper and more caring relationships. The ability to increase one's capacity to love others is a common characteristic of a wise person.

Solitude enables people to step back from their busy schedules to evaluate their priorities and goals.

29 Positive Psychology

The American economic crisis has produced a flurry of books on how Wall Street business executives speculated on the stock market and made excessively risky investments, which directly impacted the loss of American jobs. Unemployment continues to be a major social problem as several million people have lost their homes, and the short-term economic future appears bleak. People are trying to find ways to cope with these harsh realities. There are a host of self help books filled with superficial advice on thinking positive as the key to success.

A popular movement has been positive psychology that makes lofty promises about helping people, yet the psychological principles lack credible research evidence. Unfortunately, some companies will have seminars based on positive psychology that are designed to produced a manufactured happiness and social harmony. The desired effect is to reduce criticism of the organization and create more compliant employees.

> "Optimism is indeed a good thing, particularly in the pursuit of achievements, accolades, and big gains. A more pessimistic realism, on the other hand, is invaluable in pursuit of security or avoiding disastrous losses."
>
> HEIDI GRANT HALVORSON

This approach promotes a fake harmony and pressures people to display excitement when they are often feeling alienated and even inadequate. Chris Hedges notes "the loneliness of a work life where self-presentation is valued over authenticity and one must always be upbeat and positive, no matter what one's actual mood or situation, is disorienting and stressful."

Positive-psychology literature is designed to equip people to mentally dismiss negative events and to be cheerful. Those who discover they have cancer are told to focus on positive emotions and avoid being angry about their medical condition. Instead of complaining about the cancer, people should be cheerful. The absence of complaints does make life easier for the family and friends, but fails to truly help those with cancer. Barbara Ehrenreich relates "… rather than providing emotional sustenance, the sugar-coating of cancer can exact a dreadful cost."

Positive psychology encourages superficial emotions that avoid having the individual face their fears and anger. Also, constantly asking people to be positive is adding another burden to those faced with life-threatening situations. Remarkably, Deepak Chopra and other leaders of this movement continue to promote a self help philosophy stressing optimum prayer and meditation as effective ways to survive cancer. In reality, there is no research that supports a link between positive thinking and overcoming cancer. Rather, health care professionals encourage cancer patients to acknowledge their pessimistic attitudes and feelings as valid emotional responses.

Positive-psychology literature is designed to equip people to mentally dismiss negative events and to be cheerful.

The growing popularity of positive psychology is an indicator that people are searching for guidance and hope. This is a time of crisis for individuals who must live with economic uncertainty. The mass media offers plenty of options for those who are absorbed with entertainment as a way to cope with the frustration of working at a less than fulfilling job. Perhaps, individuals have fled to entertainment as a coping mechanism to handle the constant flood of negative reports about the economy and the wars in Iraq and Afghanistan.

The celebrity culture which offers entertainment to distract people from their own deeper problems also entices them to buy products beyond their means. There are growing signs that people have embraced personalities over character in selecting their leaders. Chris Hedges observes that "The consumption-oriented culture honors charm, fascination, and likeability."

There is a real need for people to develop a realistic optimism and clearly identify their goals and dreams as they construct concrete plans to reach them. The journey to reaching those dreams will require wisdom, learning to believe in themselves and cultivating healthy relationships. Family and friends can offer comfort, encouragement, affirmation and advice, while providing specific career changing assistance as well.

A classic example of having a supportive colleague is Isaac Newton. Historical records reveal that Edmond Halley, who is known for discovering Halley's Comet, played a vital role in Newton's life. There is an impressive list of ways that Halley helped Newton: he corrected mathematical errors, supplied math support for his theories, and edited and financed the printing of the book *Mathematical Principles of Natural Philosophy*. Halley's work for Newton is not well known, but his influence was significant in promoting scientific knowledge.

30 *The Rise of the Mega Church*

The past decade has witnessed the emergence of mega churches with at least 15,000 members. The churches have enormous worship services and operate fitness centers, bookstores, K-12 schools and a vast array of programs. Jesse Bogan identifies over 1,300 mega churches in the United States, and Joel Osteen's Lakewood Church in Houston, Texas has five weekly services for 43,500 people and a $80 million budget.

The church growth movement places a high priority on creating large congregations who have enormous financial resources. Church officials often claim that they do not focus on money in their ministries, yet it is hard to escape the fact these churches require massive revenue to purchase and maintain their properties and pay employees.

Unfortunately, churches have embraced the idea of being entertaining. Mega churches represent a flawed ministry model, because they rely on aggressive business principles and techniques to create large congregations. There is often an absence of a theological foundation, and though church services are appealing with contemporary music and singing, members are not challenged to make significant changes to their lives.

Too, large worship services often keep people anonymous, and this undermines individual accountability. Individuals are looking for the

> "The church is looking for better methods. God is looking for better men."
>
> E. M. BOUNDS

> The mission of the church has been blurred by leaders who promote business principles over theological studies.

church to provide guidance in handling their family problems and career issues. Yet, these religious leaders often lack sound theological training, and are not equipped to respond to deeper religious questions, often sharing advice on subjects outside of their expertise.

The mission of the church has been blurred by leaders who promote business principles over theological studies. Spirituality becomes dependent upon providing entertaining worship services that offer messages of success, prosperity and psychological comfort. A self-oriented religious philosophy is built around superficial programs and beliefs that foster cultural conformity and excessive individualism.

It is tragic to witness how ministers have trivialized God by creating a user-friendly deity who lacks mystery and transcendence. Creating the illusion of a manageable deity and the increase in social conformity are causing churches to lose both their distinctive religious mission and their influence in their local communities.

I have two graduate seminary degrees, taught numerous Sunday school classes and served as a campus minister at the University of Northern Iowa. During my life, one of my biggest disappointments has been the lack of accountability within religious institutions. Sadly, religious leaders have a tendency to cover up their mistakes by forcing people to leave their churches. I have witnessed pastors who would overlook the destructive actions of pastoral staff who were abusive toward youth. Unfortunately, churches often protect morally weak leaders who embrace these negative behaviors that undermine trust and drive people away from churches.

Ministers have embraced a business model that devalues human relationships. Church leaders are selected on the basis of their marketing ability to increase membership and create financial revenue. Those who have business degrees are chosen over those with theological education and experience. Members who have high-paying jobs are given ministry positions based on their economic value to the church's budget rather than their seasoned spirituality. The church is suffering from a major leadership crisis by focusing on cultural conformity instead of being cultural creators.

One of my major concerns about today's churches are ministers who do not study theology. There are a growing number of ministers who provide superficial *Reader's Digest* sermons that emphasize emotion and lack substance. I recall talking to my colleagues in seminary about why they were continually moving from one church to another during their career. One of the primary reasons for their church moves was their ability to re-use sermons that were prepared from their first church leadership position. Therefore, it was not some spiritual reason for leaving a church (e.g. help a new struggling church) but the motivation to avoid the study and preparation required for writing new weekly sermons.

There is a strong emphasis on having contemporary worship services and upbeat sermons that reflect more pop psychology than theology.

After visiting numerous churches and being a member of churches for many years, it is tragic for me to witness the absence of intellectual depth in the minister's Sunday messages. Pastors' failure to teach theology makes it more difficult for people to understand why they adhere to certain beliefs and doctrines (e.g. tradition). The strong emphasis on contemporary worship styles and upbeat sermons reflects more pop psychology than in-depth spiritual teaching.

American churches are failing to make a major impact on society because they reflect a deadening culture. Churches struggle in fostering authentic relationships and their talk about compassion seems quite hollow, given their meager help for the nation's poor. There is an emptiness to their enterprises that is shocking. An argument could be made that God seems to be absent from many churches because they have strayed so far from cultivating genuine believers who pursue and practice the truth.

Our nation needs religious communities that promote strong and loving relationships. People need real role models to help internalize ethical principles. Moral and emotional maturity within congregations will never occur unless their leaders become visible examples of caring and responsible behavior.

31 Where are today's leaders?

The 2010 election season witnessed both Democrat and Republican candidates trashing their opponents and claiming that they are the true leaders. Yet, neither political party has developed a relevant set of economic plans for Americans. People have grown weary of empty political promises and platitudes that lack substance.

Sadly, political leaders have relied upon short term fixes and simplistic responses to complex social problems. Now, the nation faces chronic high unemployment and an economy that is in stasis or, at best, barely growing. Economic experts often argue for more government spending to stimulate the economy, but this advice carries an assortment of financial risks that could foster even greater debts and only mildly promote economic growth.

Political leaders often devote too much time to protecting their offices through fund raising campaigns while upholding the status quo. Our federal government has grown more ineffective and wasteful of taxpayer money. Oscar Wilde once noted that "a cynic is a man who knows the price of everything and the value of nothing." Today, the national government has become a symbol of weak leaders who lack the courage to make difficult choices.

> "If I take care of my character, my reputation will take care of itself."
>
> D. L. MOODY

The recent economic crisis has placed a much larger spotlight on business executives. During the 1980s, Lee Iacocca's autobiography help promote a new kind of flamboyant and egocentric leader who seemed to be best equipped to guide large companies. Boards of directors began hiring more narcissistic people who were characterized by having an excessively positive self-regard for their talents, and an enormous need for attention and praise. Narcissistic leaders have a sense of entitlement and a willingness to use unethical business practices, which makes them vulnerable to committing white collar crimes.

The dark side of leadership is represented by individuals that rise to power and fame, but their success is built on a faulty foundation. Al Dunlap is cited by business experts as an example of an unethical leader who lied about serious financial problems at Sunbeam and emotionally abused his employees. He would establish impossible financial goals and demand that people meet them. If people complained about the unreasonable expectations, he would threaten to fire them, and this created a culture of fear. Dunlap was well-known for helping struggling companies become profitable, but his fame came at a high price. Dunlap earned the nickname "Chainsaw" because he was known for firing thousands of employees to boost stock prices.

In the book *Chainsaw: The Notorious Career of Al Dunlap in the Era of Profit-at-Any Price*, John A. Byrne paints a tragic picture of Dunlap's business behavior, "In Dunlap's presence, knees trembled and stomachs

churned. Underlings feared the torrential harangue that Dunlap could unleash at any moment. At his worst, he became viciously profane, even violent. Executives said he would throw papers or furniture, bang his hands on his desk, and shout so ferociously that a manager's hair would be blown back by the stream of air that rushed from Dunlap's mouth. 'Hair spray day' became a code phrase among execs, signifying a potential tantrum."

Business writers such as Warren Buffet and Jim Collins argue that the more effective executives focus on achieving company goals, share credit with others, and demonstrate accountability for failures and avoid seeking public praise. Our nation needs leaders who operate by humility and are driven to uphold high ethical standards. Perhaps it is time to understand the value of meekness, which is an integral part of humility.

A good definition of meekness is "power under control." The individual appreciates their own abilities but respects others and their talents. The meek person is always comfortable in different social, business and academic settings because they rejoice with others at their accomplishments and have genuine empathy for those who are experiencing difficult times. They are always learning from others and encourage people to pursue their goals and dreams. The meek are truly the difference makers in every organization. Our world needs more humble individuals who have an optimistic view of life and bring joy to others through their words and deeds.

sented by individuals that rise to
built on a faulty foundation.

32 *Conclusion*

The study of wisdom can be liberating as individuals gain greater control over their lives. Learning how to magnify our creativity and productivity is one of the exciting aspects of applying wisdom insights to our daily lives. The idea of freedom is a powerful one in the wisdom literature and in *Wonder and Critical Reflection: An Invitation to Philosophy*, Tom Christenson outlines six strategies to increase our freedom:

> "I am not afraid of tomorrow, for I have seen yesterday and I love today."
>
> WILLIAM ALLEN WHITE

❶ We may increase our freedom by becoming more aware of the means other people use to control us.

❷ We may increase our freedom when we begin to realize where our own ideas and assumptions have come from.

❸ We increase our freedom when we know or can imagine viable alternatives to the ways things are presented to us.

❹ We increase our freedom when we are able to question effectively and critique reliably those assumptions and ideas that most thoroughly 'pull our strings.'

❺ We may increase our freedom when we can plan and prioritize our lives for the long term and can actualize the skills and self-discipline necessary to act on such plans.

❻ We increase our freedom when we start to shape the things we are shaped by.

The six strategies offer a creative way to foster the freedom to live a vibrant and fulfilling life. The sixth principle challenges individuals to be cultural creators in education, business and politics. Our society needs those who are willing to use their freedom in a responsible manner to promote the common good.

Investigating wisdom has been an exciting intellectual adventure. There were times when it appeared that my thinking about the nature of wisdom had fallen into the rabbit hole of endless research studies. Writing about this complex topic has been a reminder about the literature on the virtues of patience and self-control. The wise are able to avoid the seduction of immediate gratification because they are laying the groundwork for a future that is better and more fulfilling. This mindset reflects their confidence in an accurate assessment of a brighter future. It is a form of cognitive calculating that involves having the willpower to resist being impulsive.

Life contains an assortment of decisions of varying importance. There are major decisions requiring considerable thought, such as having children, buying a home or the pursuit of a college degree. Making difficult choices is often complicated by time constraints. Stephen Hall raises an interesting perspective on the nature of wisdom: "The element of time in human decision-making, and whether making, and whether to be patient or impatient, might be viewed as the fourth dimension of wisdom." He highlights how uncertainty is a natural part of life, and points out that there are times when a quick decision is necessary and the results life-changing.

Time can create unique challenges that urge us to act by impulse to resolve an issue. This is a "seduction by short-term rewards." The ability to resist making poor choices is a theme in biblical narratives and in the lives of religious leaders through the ages. Saint Augustine wrote *Confessions* in the fifth century about an intense spiritual journey in which he developed the willpower to resist physical temptations.

There are mysteries to understanding the nature of wisdom, such as why certain individuals naturally possess greater patience. These unknowns make this a fascinating topic to study and discuss with family, co-workers and friends. Acquiring wisdom can come from painful experiences or from simply reading an insightful book.

Certain people seem to possess a unique combination of factors that promote greater self-awareness and the motivation to change and grow. The wise are good role models because they view life as an adventure, and enjoy helping others experience success.

A promising way to understand theories of wisdom is to take a comprehensive perspective. Monika Ardelt has outlined three major personality characteristics of those who possess wisdom:

1. **cognitive** - refers to the desire to know the truth and attain a deeper understanding of life, particularly with regard to intrapersonal and interpersonal matters.

2. **reflective** - represents self-examination, self-awareness, self-insight and the ability to look at phenomena and events from different perspectives.

3. **affective** - consists of a person's sympathetic and compassionate love for others.

The three characteristics are equally necessary personality components. For instance, an individual could have cognitive skills and become a successful business executive. Yet, those who are driven to obtain wealth, fame and power but lack honest self-reflection, which tends to increase their self-centered behavior and attitudes. Therefore, having only cognitive skills fails to insure the possession of wisdom. All three personality dimensions are necessary.

One of the best descriptions of a wise person comes from *Practical Wisdom: The Right Way to the Right Thing* by Barry Schwartz and Kenneth Sharpe:

❶ A wise person knows the proper aims of the activity she is engaged in. She wants to do the right thing to achieve these aims, to meet the needs of the people she is serving.

❷ A wise person knows how to improvise, balancing conflicting aims and interpreting rules and principles in light of each specific context.

❸ A wise person is perceptive, knows how to read a social context, and knows how to move beyond the black-and-white of rules and see the gray in each situation.

❹ A wise person knows how to take on the perspective of another—to see the situation as the other person does and thus to understand how the other feels. This perspective-taking is what enables a wise person to feel empathy for others and to make decisions that serve the client's (student's, patient's, friend's) needs.

❺ A wise person knows how to make emotion an ally of reason, to rely on emotion to signal what a situation calls for, and to inform judgment without distorting it. He intuitively feels, or 'just knows' what the right thing to do is, enabling him to act quickly when timing matters. Both his emotions and intuitions are well educated.

❻ A wise person is an experienced person. Practical wisdom is a craft, and craftsmen are trained by having the right experiences. People learn how to be brave, said Aristotle, by doing brave things. This is true of honesty, justice, loyalty, caring, listening, and counseling as well.

So, we have presented a description of what we might aim for as we seek wisdom, as we seek to live as a wise person. This book has described research into this fascinating subject involving a diversity of academic disciplines. The narrative has discussed the nature of wisdom while offering relevant ways to acquire and apply wisdom in our daily lives. The ability to approach and solve problems creatively reflects one of the many benefits of wisdom.

I wish you much success in your endeavors and the blessings that come from making wise decisions.

The ability to approach and solve problems creatively reflects one of the many benefits of wisdom.

Notes

Chapter One: What is wisdom?

Hall, S. (2010). *Wisdom: From Philosophy to Neuroscience.* New York,NY: Alfred A. Knopf, p. 142.

Chapter Two: Encouraging Creativity

Kaufman, J. C. & Sternberg, R. J. (2007). Resource review: Creativity. *Change,* 39 (4), p.55.

Morris, W. (2006). Creativity: It's place in education. Available: http://www.jpb.com/creative/Creativity_in_Education. pdf, p.5.

Weisburg, R. W. (2006). *Creativity: Understanding innovation in problem solving, science, invention, and the arts.* Hoboken, NJ: John Wiley & Sons, p. 100.

Sternberg, R. J. (2010). *College admissions for 21st century.* Cambridge, MA: Harvard University Press, p. 53.

Chapter Three: Creativity Challenges In Education

Makel, M. C. (2009). Help us researchers, you're are only hope. *Psychology of Aesthetics, Creativity, and the Arts,* 3(1), p.39.

Schwartz, B. & Sharpe, K. (2010). *Practical wisdom: The right way to do the right thing.* New York, NY: Riverhead Books, p. 169.

Gatto, J. T. (2010). *Weapons of mass instruction: A school teacher's journey through the dark world of compulsory schooling.* Gabriola Island, BC: New Society Publishers, p. xvii.

Beghetto, R. A. (2007). *Ideational code-switching: Walking the talk about supporting student creativity in the classroom. Roeper Review,* 29 (4), p. 265.

Makel, M. C. (2009). Help us researchers, you're our only hope. *Psychology of Aesthetics, Creativity, and the Arts,* 3(1), p.39.

Kaufman, J. C., & Beghetto, R. A. (2009). Beyond big and little: The Four C Model of Creativity. *Review of General Psychology,* 13, 1-12.

Levy, D. A. (2010). *Tools of critical thinking: Metathoughts for psychology,* (2nd ed.). Long Grove, IL: Waveland Press, p. 5.

Sternberg, R. J., Lubart, T. I., Kaufman, J. C., & Pretz, J. E. (2005). Creativity (Ch. 15). In Holyoak, K. J., & Morrison, R. G. (Eds.), *The Cambridge handbook of thinking and reasoning.* New York: Cambridge University Press, p. 358.

Chapter Four: Improving Creativity

Harris, R. (1998). Introduction to creative thinking. Available from http://www.virtualsalt.com/crebook1.htm, para#2, 4-5.

Amabile, T. M. (1998). How to kill creativity. *Harvard Business Review,* 76 (5), 76-87.

Breen, B. (2004, December) The 6 myths of creativity. *Fast Company,* pp.75-78.

Chapter Five: Becoming Indispensable

Hallinan, J. T. (2009). *Why we make mistakes: How we look without seeing, forget things in seconds, and are all pretty sure we are above average.* New York, NY: Broadway Books, p. 5.

Chapter Eight: Helping Others

Roberts, R. C. & Wood, W. J. (2007). *Intellectual virtues: An essay in regulative epistemology.* Oxford, England: Oxford University Press, p. 286.

Maxwell, J. (2004). *Today matters.* New York, NY: Time Warner Book Group, p. 227.

Chapter Nine: Setting Goals

Reeve, J. M. (2005). *Understanding motivation and emotion* (4th ed.). Hobokenm NJ: John Wiley & Sons, p. 207.

Chapter Ten: Encouraging People's Dreams

Maxwell, J. & Parrot, L. (2005). *25 ways to win with people.* Nashville, TN: Thomas Nelson, p. 57.

Chapter Eleven: Why is it difficult to learn from mistakes?

Maxwell, J. (2000). *Failing forward: Turning mistakes into stepping stones.* Nashville, TN: Thomas Nelson, pp. 155-163.

Tugend, A. (2011). *Better by mistake: The unexpected benefits of being wrong.* New York, NY: Riverhead Publishing, p. 20.

Schoemaker, P. J. H., & Gunther, R. E. (2006). The wisdom of deliberate mistakes. *Harvard Business Review,* 84 (6), p. 111.

Chapter Twelve: The Value of Pessimism

Scruton, R. (2010). *The uses of pessimism.* Oxford: Oxford University Press, p. 22.

Maxwell, J. (2002). *Your road map for success.* Nashville, TN: Thomas Nelson, 98-105.

Chapter Thirteen: Dealing With Uncertainty

Hall, S. (2010). *Wisdom: From Philosophy to Neuroscience.* New York, NY: Alfred A. Knopf, p. 193.

Hall, S. (2010). *Wisdom: From Philosophy to Neuroscience.* New York, NY: Alfred A. Knopf, p. 60.

Chapter Fourteen: Boring Education

Gatto, J. T. (1992). *Dumbing us down: The hidden curriculum of compulsory schooling.* Philadelphia, PA: New Society Publishers.

Kohn, A. (2011). *Feel-bad education and other contrarian essays on children and schooling.* Boston, MA: Beacon Press, p. 149.

Blackburn, S. (2009). *The big questions: Philosophy.* New York, NY: Metro Books, p. 158.

Chapter Fifteen: Meaningful Learning

Dewey, J. (1916). *Democracy and Education: An Introduction to Philosophy of Education.* New York, NY: Macmillan, p. 158.

Chapter Sixteen: Teachers

Hargreaves, A. (1995). Realities of teaching. In L.W. Anderson (Ed.)., *International encyclopedia of teaching and teacher education* (2nd ed., pp. 80-87). Tarry Town, NY: Elsevier Science, p. 80.

Godin, S. (2009). *Linchpin: Are you indispensable?* New York: Portfolio Publishers, p. 29.

Chapter Eighteen: Higher Education

White, F. (2008). *The daily writer: 366 mediations to cultivate productive and meaningful writing.* Cincinnati, OH: Writer's Digest Books, p. 181.

Chapter Nineteen: Online University Dialogs

Furedi, F. (2004). *Where have all the intellectuals gone? Confronting 21st century philistinism.* New York, NY: Continuum, p.138.

Chapter Twenty: Doctoral Studies

Menand, L. (2010). *The marketplace of ideas: Reform and resistance in the American University.* New York, NY: W. W. Norton & Company, p. 152.

Chapter Twenty-One: Writing Skills

Ray, D. S. (2010). Freelance article writing: Tips for establishing and maintaining good relationships with magazine editors. Available from: http://www.sawn.co.za/magtips.htm, para#4.

Chapter Twenty-Two: Creative Writing

Plotnik, A. (2007). *Spunk & bite: A writer's guide to bold, contemporary style.* New York: Random House, p. 77.

Wilbers, S. (2000). *Keys to writing.* Cincinnati, OH: Writer's Digest Books, p. 124.

Imber, A. (Spring, 2011). Predicting the unpredictable. *Fast Thinking,* 82-83.

Sternberg, R. J. (2010). *College admissions for 21st century.* Cambridge, MA: Harvard University Press, p. 155.

Chapter Twenty-Three: Science Fiction Insights

Moskowitz, S. (1963). *Explorers of the Infinite: Shapers of Science Fiction.* Cleveland, OH: Meridian Books, p. 138.

Prucher, J. (2009). *Brave new words: The Oxford dictionary of science fiction.* Oxford, England: Oxford University Press, p. 39.

Bradbury, R. (1953). *Fahrenheit 451.* New York, NY: Random House, p. 106.

McCurdy, H. E. (2006). Vision and leadership: The view from science fiction. *Public Integrity,* 8(3), p. 268.

Chapter Twenty-Four: Blogs

Jarret, T. (2003). What is a blog? Available from http://www.jarretthousenorth.com/2003/10/10.html#a2781, para#2.

Chapter Twenty-Five: Blog Popularity

Farrell, H. (2005, December 7). The blogosphere as a carnival of ideas. *The Chronicle Review,* 52 (7), p. B14.

Downes, S. (2004). Educational blogging. *Educause Review,* 39 (5), p. 18.

Phillips, K. (2008, October, 19). Obama raised over $150 million in September. New York Times. Available from http://thecaucus.blogs.nytimes.com/2008/10/19/obama-raised-record-150-million-in-september/

Bar-tura, A. (2010). Wall to wall or face to face. In Wittkower, D. E. (Ed.) *Facebook and philosophy: What is on your mind?* (231-239). Chicago, IL: Open Court Publishing, p. 239.

Chapter Twenty-Six: Childrens' Television Shows

Harris, R. J. (2004). *A cognitive psychology of mass communication* (4th ed.). Mahwah, NJ: Lawrence Erlbaum Associates, p. 125.

Bryant, J. & Zillman, D. (Eds.). (2002). *Media effects: Advances in theory and research.* Mahwah, NJ: Lawrence Erlbaum Associates, p. 273.

Chapter Twenty-Eight: Social Conformity

Lipman, M. (1995). Critical thinking - what can it be? In A. L. Ornstein & L. S. Behar (Eds.) *Contemporary Issues in Curriculum,* Boston, MA: Allyn Bacon, p. 146.

Guiness, O. (1994). *Fit bodies Fat minds.* Grand Rapids, MI: Baker Books, pp. 78-79.

White, C. (2003). *The middle mind: Why Americans don't think for themselves.* San Francisco, CA: HarperCollins, p.10.

Chapter Twenty-Nine: Positive Psychology

Hedges, C. (2009). *Empire of illusion: The end of literacy and the triumph of spectacle.* New York, NY: Nation Books, pp. 138-139.

Ehrenreich, B. (2009). *Bright-sided: How positive thinking is undermining America.* New York, NY: Picador, p. 41.

Hedges, C. (2009). *Empire of illusion: The end of literacy and the triumph of spectacle.* New York, NY: Nation Books, p. 51.

Chapter Thirty-One: Where Are Today's Leaders

Byrne, J. A. (1999). *Chainsaw: The notorious career of Al Dunlap in the era of profit-at-any price.* New York, NY: HarperBusiness, p. 135.

Chapter Thirty-Two: Conclusion

Christenson, T. (2001). *Wonder and critical reflection: An invitation to philosophy.* Upper Saddle Creek, NJ: Prentice-Hall, pp. 77-82.

Hall, S. (2010). *Wisdom: From Philosophy to Neuroscience.* New York, NY: Alfred A. Knopf, p. 178.

Ainslie, G. (2001). *Breakdown of the will.* Cambridge, U.K: Cambridge University Press, p. 178.

Ardelt, M. (2004).Wisdom as expert knowledge system: A critical review of a contemporary operationalization of an ancient concept. *Human Development,* 47(5), pp. 275-276.

Schwartz, B. & Sharpe, K. (2010). *Practical wisdom: The right way to do the right thing.* New York, NY: Riverhead Books, pp. 25-26.

Bibliography

Ainslie, G. (2001). *Breakdown of the will*. Cambridge, U.K: Cambridge University Press.

Amabile, T. M. (1998). How to kill creativity. *Harvard Business Review,* 76 (5), 76-87.

Anderson, J. R. (2005). *Cognitive psychology and its implications* (6th Ed.), New York, NY: Worth Publishers.

Anderson, N. (2004). *Work with passion: How to do what you love for a living* (Rev.). Novato, CA: New World Library.

Ardelt, M. (2004).Wisdom as expert knowledge system: A critical review of a contemporary operationalization of an ancient concept. *Human Development,* 47(5), 257-285.

Bakewell, S. (2010). *A life of Montaigne: In one question and twenty attempts at an answer.* Esses, U.K. Random House.

Barber, T. (2010). *The inspiration factor. How you can revitalize your company in 12 weeks.* Austin, TX: Greenleaf Book Group Press.

Bar-tura, A. (2010). Wall to wall or face to face. In Wittkower, D. E. (Ed.) *Facebook and philosophy: What is on your mind?* (231-239). Chicago, IL: Open Court Publishing.

Beghetto, R. A. (2010). Creativity in the classroom. In J. C. Kaufman & R. J. Sternberg (Eds.), *The Cambridge Handbook of Creativity* (447-463). New York, NY: Cambridge University Press.

Beghetto, R. A. (2007). Ideational code-switching: Walking the talk about supporting student creativity in the classroom. *Roeper Review,* 29 (4), 265-270.

Beghetto, R. A. & Plucker, J. A. (2006). The relationship among schooling, learning and creativity: "All roads lead to creativity" or "You can't get there from here"? In James C. Kaufman & John Baer (Eds.),

Creativity and reason in cognitive development (316-332). New York, NY: Cambridge University Press.

Bensha, N. (2009). *The journey to greatness.* Thousand Oaks, CA. Corwin Press.

Blackburn, S. (2009). *The big questions: Philosophy.* New York,NY: Metro Books.

Bogan, J. (2009). America's biggest megachurches. Available from http://www.forbes.com/2009/06/26/americas-biggest-megachurches-business-megachurches.html

Boggs, J. M. & Petrie, D. W. (2004). *The art of watching films,* 6th ed. Boston, MA: McGrawHill.

Booker, M. K. (2008). Science fiction and the cold war. In Seed, D. (Ed.). *A companion to science fiction,* 171-184. Malden, MA: Blackwell Publishing.

Bradbury, R. (1953). *Fahrenheit 451.* New York, NY: Random House.

Branford, J. D. Brown, A. L., & Cocking, R. R. (Eds.). (2000). *How people learn: Brain, mind, experience, and school.* Washington, D.C.: National Academy Press.

Breen, B. (2004, December) The 6 myths of creativity. *Fast Company,* 75-78.

Bruning, R. H., Schraw, G. J., Norby, M. N., & Ronning, R. R. (2004). *Cognitive psychology and instruction* (4th Ed.), Upper Saddle River, NJ: Pearson.

Bryant, J. & Zillman, D. (Eds.). (2002). *Media effects: Advances in theory and research.* Mahwah, NJ: Lawrence Erlbaum Associates.

Byrne, J. A. (1999). *Chainsaw: The notorious career of Al Dunlap in the era of profit-at-any price.* New York: HarperBusiness.

Carson, S. (2010). *Your creative brain: Seven steps to maximize imagination, productivity and innovation in your life.* San Francisco, CA: Jossey-Bass.

Christenson, T. (2001). *Wonder and critical reflection: An invitation to philosophy.* Upper Saddle Creek, NJ: Prentice-Hall.

Collison, G., Elbaum, Haavind, S., & Tinker, R. (2000). *Facilitating online learning. Effective strategies for moderators.* Madison, WI: Atwood Publishing

Colvin, G. (2008). *Talent is overrated: What really separates world-class performers from everybody else.* New York, NY: Penguin Group.

Csikszentmihalyi, M. (1996). *Creativity: The flow of psychology of discovery and invention,* New York, NY: HarperCollins.

Cuddon, J. A. (1998). Science Fiction. *Dictionary of literary terms and literary theory* (4th ed.). London, England: Penguin Books.

Culley, A. (2007). Mindtools. Available from http://instructionaldesign.com.au/Academic/mindtools.htm

Delaney, C. F. (1999). Dewey, John. Audi, R. (Gen. Ed.). *The Cambridge Dictionary of Philosophy* (2nd ed)., 229-231. Cambridge, England: Cambridge University Press.

Dewey, J. (1916). *Democracy and Education: An Introduction to Philosophy of Education.* New York, NY: Macmillan.

Downes, S. (2004). Educational blogging. *Educause Review,* 39 (5), 14-26.

Ehrenreich, B. (2009). *Bright-sided: How positive thinking is undermining America.* New York, NY: Picador.

Farrell, H. (2005, December 7). The blogosphere as a carnival of ideas. *The Chronicle Review,* 52 (7), B14.

Fisch, S. M. (2002). Vast wasteland or vast opportunity? Effects of educational television on children's academic knowledge, skills and attitudes. In Bryant, J. & Zillmann, D. (Eds.). *Media effects: advances in theory and research,* (2nd ed.) pp. 397-426. Mahwah, NJ: Lawrence Erlbaum Associates.

Fullan, M. (2007). *The new meaning of educational change* (4th ed.). New York, NY: Teachers College.

Furedi, F. (2004). *Where have all the intellectuals gone? Confronting 21st century philistinism.* New York, NY: Continuum.

Gatto, J. T. (2010). *Weapons of mass instruction: A school teacher's journey through the dark world of compulsory schooling.* Gabriola Island, BC: New Society Publishers.

Gatto, J. T. (1992). *Dumbing us down: The hidden curriculum of compulsory schooling.* Philadelphia, PA: New Society Publishers.

Godin, S. (2009). *Linchpin: Are you indispensable?* New York, NY: Portfolio Publishers.

Grigorenko, E. L., & Sternberg, R. J. (1997). Styles of thinking, abilities, and academic performance. *Exceptional Children,* 63(3), 295-312.

Guilford, J. P. (1975). Varieties of creative giftedness, their measurement and development. Gifted Child Quarterly, 16(2), 175-184, 239-243.

Guiness, O. (1994). *Fit bodies Fat minds.* Grand Rapids, MI: Baker Books.

Guinness, O. & Seel, J. (1992). *No God but God: Breaking with the idols of our age.* Chicago, IL: Moody Press.

Hacker, A. & Dreifus, C. (2010). *Higher education?: How colleges are wasting our money and failing our kids—and what we can do about it.* New York, NY: Times Books.

Hall, S. (2010). *Wisdom: From Philosophy to Neuroscience.* New York, NY: Alfred A. Knopf.

Halpern, D. F. (1996). *Knowledge & thought: An introduction to critical thinking.* Mahwah, NJ: Lawrence Erlbaum Associates.

Hallinan, J. T. (2009). *Why we make mistakes: How we look without seeing, forget things in seconds, and are all pretty sure we are above average.* New York, NY: Broadway Books.

Hargreaves, A. (1995). Realities of teaching. In L.W. Anderson (Ed.)., *International encyclopedia of teaching and teacher education* (2nd ed., pp. 80-87). Tarry Town, NY: Elsevier Science.

Harris, R. J. (2004). A cognitive psychology of mass communication (4th ed.). Mahwah, NJ: Lawrence Erlbaum Associates.

Harris, R. (1998). Introduction to creative thinking. Available from http://www.virtualsalt.com/crebook1.htm.

Haynes, N. (2010). *Ancient guide to modern life.* New York, NY: The Overlook Press.

Hedges, C. (2009). *Empire of illusion: The end of literacy and the triumph of spectacle.* New York, NY: Nation Books.

Henson, K. T. (1999). *Writing for professional publication: Keys to academic and business success.* Boston, MA: Allyn & Bacon.

Hinman, L. M. (2002). Telling like it is: Lying on your resume. Available from http://ethics.sandiego.edu/resources/cases/Detail.asp?ID=90

Howe, M. J. A. (1999). *Genius explained,* Cambridge, England: Cambridge University Press.

Imber, A. (Spring, 2011). *Predicting the unpredictable.* Fast Thinking, 80-83.

Jarret, T. (2003). What is a blog? Available from http://www.jarretthousenorth.com/2003/10/10.html#a2781

Jaschik, S. (2009, March 13). Top Ph.D. programs, shrinking. *Inside Higher Education.* Available from http://www.insidehighered.com/news/2009/05/13/doctoral

Kaufman, J. C. & Beghetto, R. A. (2009). Beyond big and little: The four C model of creativity. *Review of General Psychology,* 13 (1), 1-12.

Kaufman, J. C. & Sternberg, R. J. (2007). Resource review: Creativity. *Change,* 39 (4), 55-58.

King, S. (2000). *On writing: A memoir of the craft.* New York, NY: Charles Scribner's Sons.

Kohn, A. (2011). *Feel-bad education and other contrarian essays on children and schooling.* Boston, MA: Beacon Press.

Levy, D. A. (2010). *Tools of critical thinking: Metathoughts for psychology,* (2nd ed.). Long Grove, IL: Waveland Press.

Lipman, M. (1995). Critical thinking - what can it be? In A. L. Ornstein & L. S. Behar (Eds.) *Contemporary Issues in Curriculum,* Boston, MA: Allyn Bacon, 145-152.

Litt, T. (2009). Out of this word. *New Statesman,* 138 (4967), 47-48.

Lubart, T. I., & Sternberg, R. J. (1995). An investment approach to creativity: Theory and data. In S. M. Smith, T. B. Ward, & R. A. Finke (Eds.), *The creative cognition approach* (pp. 269–302). Cambridge, MA: MIT Press.

Maddi, S. R. & Khoshaba, D. M. (2005). *Resilience at work: How to succeed no matter what life throws at you.*

Makel, M. C. (2009). Help us researchers, you're our only hope. *Psychology of Aesthetics, Creativity, and the Arts,* 3(1), 38-42.

Maxwell, J. (2007). *The Maxwell Daily Reader.* Nashville,TN: Thomas Nelson.

Maxwell, J. & Parrot, L. (2005). *25 ways to win with people.* Nashville, TN: Thomas Nelson.

Maxwell, J. (2004). *Today matters.* New York, NY: Time Warner Book Group.

Maxwell, J. (2002). *Your road map for success.* Nashville, TN: Thomas Nelson.

Maxwell, J. (2000). *Failing forward: Turning mistakes into stepping stones.* Nashville, TN: Thomas Nelson.

McCullough, D. W. (1995). *The trivialization of God: The dangerous illusion of manageable deity.* Colorado Springs, CO: NavPress.

McCurdy, H. E. (2006). Vision and leadership: The view from science fiction. *Public Integrity,* 8(3), 257-270.

Menand, L. (2010). *The marketplace of ideas: Reform and resistance in the American University.* New York, NY: W. W. Norton & Company.

Merriam, J. (1996). *A history of modern Europe: From the Renaissance to the present.* New York, NY: W.W. Norton.

Miller, J. (2011). *Examined lives: From Socrates to Nietzsche.* New York, NY: Farrar, Straus and Giroux.

Morris, W. (2006). Creativity: Its place in education. Available: http://www.jpb.com/creative/Creativity_in_Education.pdf

Moskowitz, S. (1963). *Explorers of the Infinite: Shapers of Science Fiction.* Cleveland, OH: Meridian Books.

Muirhead, B. (2008). *A reader in online education.* Minneapolis, MN: Mill City Press.

Parkhurst, H. B. (1999). Confusion, lack of consensus, and definitions of creativity as a construct. *Journal of Creative Behavior,* 33(1), 1-21.

Phillips, D. C. (2006). Theories of teaching and learning. Curran, R. (Ed.). *A companion to the philosophy of education.* 232-245. Oxford, England: Blackwell Publishing.

Phillips, K. (2008, October, 19). Obama raised over $150 million in September. New York Times. Available from http://thecaucus.blogs.nytimes.com/2008/10/19/obama-raised-record-150-million-in-september/

Phillips, P. (2007). *Socrates in love: Philosophy for a passionate heart.* New York, NY: W. W. Norton & Company.

Pipher, M. (2006). *Writing to change the world.* New York, NY: Riverhead Books.

Plotnik, A (2007). *Spunk & bite: A writer's guide to bold, contemporary style.* New York, NY: Random House.

Prucher, J. (2009). *Brave new words: The Oxford dictionary of science fiction.* Oxford, England: Oxford University Press.

Quinn, E. (2006). *Literary and thematic terms* (2nd ed.). New York, NY: Checkmark Books.

Ravitch, D. (2010). *The death and life of the great American school system: How testing and choice are undermining education.* New York, NY: Basic Books.

Ray, D. S. (2010). Freelance article writing: Tips for establishing and maintaining good relationships with magazine editors. Available from: http://www.sawn.co.za/magtips.htm

Reeve, J. M. (2005). *Understanding motivation and emotion* (4th ed.). Hobokenm, NJ: John Wiley & Sons.

Richardson, R. D. (2009). *First we read, then we write.* Iowa City, IA: University of Iowa Press.

Richardson, W. (2006). *Blogs, wikis, podcasts, and other powerful web tools for classrooms.* Thousand Oaks, CA: Corwin Press.

Roberts, R. C. & Wood, W. J. (2007). *Intellectual virtues: An essay in regulative epistemology.* Oxford, England: Oxford University Press.

Royal, B. (2004). *The little red writing book.* Cincinnati, OH: Writer's Digest Books.

Tugend, A. (2011). *Better by mistake: The unexpected benefits of being wrong.* New York, NY: Riverhead Books.

Sawyer, R. K. (2006). *Explaining creativity: The science of human innovation,* Oxford, England: Oxford University Press.

Schacter, D. L. (2001). *The seven sins of memory: How the mind forgets and remembers.* New York, NY: Houghton Mifflin.

Schacter, D. L. (2001a). *The seven sins of memory. Psychology Today,* 34 (3), 62-66,87.

Schacter, D. L. (1996). *Searching for memory: The brain, the mind, and the past,* New York, NY: Basic Books.

Schacter, J., Thum, Y. M. & Zifklin, D. (2006). How much does creative teaching enhance elementary school students' achievement? *Journal of Creative Behavior,* 40 (1), 47-72

Schoemaker, P. J. H., & Gunther, R. E. (2006). The wisdom of deliberate mistakes. *Harvard Business Review,* 84 (6), 108-115.

Schwartz, B. & Sharpe, K. (2010). *Practical wisdom: The right way to do the right thing.* New York, NY: Riverhead Books.

Scruton, R. (2010). *The uses of pessimism.* Oxford: Oxford University Press.

Simon, L. (2004). William James, Popular Intellectual. In (Lamb. B. Ed.). *Booknotes on American character.* New York, NY: Public Affairs, 481-487.

Smith, J. K. & Smith, L. F. (2010). Educational creativity. In J.C. Kaufman & R. J. Sternberg (Eds.), *The Cambridge Handbook of Creativity* (250-264). New York,NY: Cambridge University Press.

Schwartz, B. & Sharpe, K. (2010). *Practical wisdom: The right way to do the right thing.* New York: Riverhead Books.

Sternberg, R. J. (2010). *College admissions for 21st century.* Cambridge, MA: Harvard University Press.

Sternberg, R. J., Lubart, T. I., Kaufman, J. C., & Pretz, J. E. (2005). Creativity (Ch. 15). In Holyoak, K. J., & Morrison, R. G. (Eds.), *The Cambridge handbook of thinking and reasoning.* New York: Cambridge University Press, 351-369.

Sternberg, R. J. (2003). Creative thinking in the classroom. *Scandinavian Journal of Educational Research,* 47 (3), 325-338.

Strunk, W. & White, E. B. (1999). *The elements of style* (4th ed.). Upper Saddle River, NJ: Longman Publishing.

Torrance, E. P. (1972). Can we teach children think creatively? *Journal of Creative Behavior,* 6, 114-143

Travis, C. & Aronson, E. (2007). *Mistakes were made (But not by me).* Chicago, IL: Houghton Mifflin Harcourt.

Tugend, A. (2011). *Better by mistake: The unexpected benefits of being wrong.* New York, NY: Riverhead Publishing.

Twenge, J. M., & Campbell, W. K. (2009). *The narcissism epidemic: Living in the age of entitlement.* New York, NY: Free Press.

Weisburg, R. W. (2006). *Creativity: Understanding innovation in problem solving, science, invention, and the arts.* Hoboken, NJ: John Wiley & Sons.

White, C. (2003). *The middle mind: Why Americans don't think for themselves.* San Francisco, CA: HarperCollins.

White, F. (2008). *The daily writer: 366 mediations to cultivate productive and meaningful writing.* Cincinnati, OH: Writer's Digest Books.

Wilbers, S. (2000). *Keys to writing.* Cincinnati, OH: Writer's Digest Books.

Wilheim, T. (2008). High-fidelity, creative teaching. *Leadership,* 38 (27), 32-36.

Wood, W. J. & Roberts, R. C. (2007). *Intellectual virtues: An essay in regulative epistemology.* Oxford, England: Oxford University Press.

Yang, S. Y. (2008). A process view of wisdom. *Journal of Adult Development,* 15(2), 62-75.

Zorana, I. (2009). Creativity map: Toward the next generation of theories of creativity. *Psychology of Aesthetics, Creativity, and the Arts,* 3(1), 17-21.

www.ingramcontent.com/pod-product-compliance
Lightning Source LLC
Chambersburg PA
CBHW042349300426
44109CB00035B/134